THE

PRESENCE BASED
CHURCH

TERRY TEYKL
LYNN PONDER

Prayer Point Press

The Presence Based Church
Copyright © 2003 Dr. Terry Teykl
Published by Prayer Point Press

Fourth Printing, December 2005

ISBN: 1-57892-112-0
Printed in the United States of America

Prayer Point Press
2100 N. Carrolton Dr.
Muncie, IN 47304
Phone: (765) 759-0215
To order, call toll free: (888) 656-6067
or visit www.prayerpointpress.com

To Mike James, long-time friend and supporter who taught me how to love and appreciate the people of Israel.

CONTENTS

O God and Father, I repent of my sinful preoccupation
with visible things.
The world has been too much with me.
Thou hast been here and I knew it not.
I have been blind to Thy presence.
Open my eyes that I may behold Thee in and around me.
For Christ's sake, Amen.[1]

INTRODUCTION

I'm a simple man. I don't think of myself as a great Bible scholar or intellectual theologian. I also think God must agree, because when he shows me things, they tend to be simple. Fascinatingly simple.

I remember the day I was driving through East Texas thinking as I often do, and I saw two circles in my mind. The two circles represented two different kinds of churches. In the middle of one circle was the word "God" and in the middle of the other circle was the word "people." It was simple, and yet profoundly revelatory to me at that moment because I knew the Lord was showing me something that would germinate and grow.

Today, as I held the nearly completed manuscript in my hands for the first time, I had to cry. Although this isn't my first book, I never get over the wonder of how a prolific and fruitful tree comes from such a tiny seed.

I have tried to write about the Presence of God, well aware that it's a topic I will never feel I did justice to. The Presence of God is simply bigger than my vocabulary, bigger than my experience, even bigger than my imagination. Yet, it has intrigued me from the early days of my ministry. Highlighted throughout my very first Bible is passage after passage describing the Presence of God—how and when he revealed himself, the relationship he had with his creation, what his Presence felt like and looked like to those who experienced it.

As a pastor for 28 years I learned some things about his Presence. I learned that it was my only hope with a new church plant in a college town. I learned to recognize when it was there and when it wasn't. I learned that it often made people cry and that it always made a difference. I learned that I couldn't control it, but I could influence it. Most importantly, I learned that doing church without it was ridiculous and always led to trouble, if not sooner, then later.

Most of the books I have written relate to prayer. Actually, all of them do. So this book has been an exciting deviation from the norm for me. Yet, it has been my keen awareness of the necessity of the Presence of God in church life that has driven my passion to pray and to "build the church in prayer." The house of prayer is built for the Presence of God to dwell in—not visit or look at, but actually inhabit. Prayer invites the Holy Spirit to come, and somehow keeps us from wandering into self-indulgent, irrelevant territory. Prayer has everything to do with the Presence of God, and the Presence of God unfolds in answer to prayer.

Not Another Model

When it comes to doing church today, pastors have a buffet of church models to choose from—each one promising to build a healthy, growing church. It's hard to say how many models there really are, because even the experts would come up with slightly different lists. Here are six I consider distinctive:

The Cell Based Church – strives to plug people into personal relationships with one another through small groups, often connected by a common interest (known as "free-market cells"). This model—born of Weslyan heritage—has flourished under such pastors as Ralph Neighbor, Paul Cho and Ted Haggard.

The Purpose Driven Church – based on defining and communicating the church's vision and activity around the five biblical purposes for the church: outreach, worship, fellowship, discipleship and service. This model was developed by Rick Warren primarily out of his experience as the pastor of Saddleback Valley Community Church in Orange County, California.

The Program Based Church – thrives on offering a wide variety of activities, classes, ministries and services to appeal to as many different people/age groups within the community as possible.

The Apostolic Church – characterized by its apostolic leadership style that gives visionary pastors the freedom to lead, without the constraints of institutionalism. This church model came out of the 90's explosion of independent, charismatic (though not exclusively) megachurches and was named by C. Peter Wagner.

The Traditional Church – built on the established structure, liturgy, theology and heritage of the major mainline denominations such as Baptist, United Methodist, Episcopal, Lutheran, Presbyterian and Assemblies of God.

The Seeker Church – tailors the weekend church service around the perceived needs, preferences and desires of "seekers"—those who are unchurched and/or presumably unsaved—with the goal of enticing them into church life. Pastor Bill Hybels of Willow Creek Community Church in the Chicago area is credited with developing and perfecting this model.

The Meatloaf Church – creates its own flavor by mixing a little of this model with a little of that. It is, of course, not actually a church model, but is worth mentioning since most congregations are actually hybrids of these concepts.

Every one of these church types has something to offer the body of Christ, and hundreds of churches are better and stronger because of their strategies and ideas. I applaud the pastors who were bold enough to step beyond yesterday's successes to embrace new visions, and I respect the ones that have helped preserve our spiritual history, both as Christians and Americans.

These models however, any one of which can be dynamic and successful or dismal and empty, have to do with organizational structure, leadership, style preference and programs. The Presence based church, on the other hand, is about whether or not Jesus factors into these areas and to what extent. Is he the Master or the mascot? Does he receive our unbridled worship and adoration or just our requests and complaints? Is he the honored guest at all of our functions, or do we esteem people above all and relegate him to the role of butler? Is he the hope of glory or the hood ornament?

I realize that some people who read this book may see it as another model—just another menu item to add to the list. But that is not my intent. Although it does have some distinctive characteristics, the Presence based church is not a model that can be implemented through education or training. It is not a program that can be bought or copied. There are no sequential steps to follow, and no master plan. More importantly, there is no reason that the Presence based church can not coexist and enhance any or all of these various models.

Here's the hard truth—in many churches today, the Presence of God is absent. He doesn't sign the attendance book on Sunday and he's on the inactive roll. The people show up to fill a seat and take advantage of programs tailored to their needs that are wholesome yet spiritually neutered. They never experience the Presence of God, and in fact they haven't experienced it in so long, if ever, that they don't even know it's missing. If they did, they might not care. The Presence of God is not necessarily welcome or essential for this kind of institution to operate.

This is a picture of what I call the *consumer* based church, today's market-driven mutant of what church is supposed to be. Influenced heavily by the corporate world and driven by large budgets and fierce competition, these churches fight for their market share of members through advertising, programming and image control. With spiritual CEO's at the helm, their goal is to offer the most enticing product at the right price. The unwritten slogan: Get them in the door and do whatever it takes to keep them coming back.

The Presence Based Church

I love the local church. It is God's hope for transformation of lives, the expression of his glory in the earth, and his chosen bride for the Son. If someone today wants to sense and experience the real and manifested Presence of God, he shouldn't have to go any further than the local church on the corner. Revivals are fine; special events are wonderful; and crusades are exciting. But the local church should be the ongoing, steady flame of his Presence, kept alive by the worship and prayer of believers.

Regardless of size, style or label, any church can become more Presence based than it already is. The Presence of God just makes everything about a church work better! It will make the apostolic leader a world changer; it will cause seekers to thirst for truth; it will turn every cell group into a spiritual oasis; and it will lead congregations and individuals to fulfill their kingdom purposes.

As the body of Christ, we desperately need the Presence of God. We are nothing without it. His Presence, unrivaled in any aspect of beauty, power, fame or majesty, is our provision and glory. It should be the thing that holds us up and sets us apart. One moment in the Presence can do more than a lifetime of church services without it. I pray that you will find more of his Presence than you have known before, and discover the joy of being a Presence based church.

T HE M ARTHA
C HURCH

T hirty people for dinner! That's what Martha was thinking about that afternoon, having invited Jesus and his disciples to come to her home to eat and rest. Martha loved to entertain, especially someone as notable as Jesus. (If she were alive today, her last name might be "Stewart.") She no doubt scurried around the small house—she didn't have much time—cleaning and attending to every last detail to make her guests feel at home. She may have even sent Mary, her sister, to the market for a special jug of wine or more flour. She took pride in her ability to perform under pressure, keep things under control and running smoothly. That was Martha. She wanted everything to be just right, as it always was.

When Jesus arrived, I imagine she politely stepped out of

the kitchen, wiping her hands and face and straightening her apron, to welcome them in before excusing herself back to the stove where large simmering pots were giving off savory aromas. There was still so much to be done. Luke remembers that Martha was "distracted by all the preparations that had to be made" (Luke 10:39).

As the guests settled in the main room of the house, Mary felt a twinge of guilt for not excusing herself as well to help Martha in the kitchen. Nevertheless she could not tear herself away from Jesus' presence. She sat at his feet, longingly soaking up every word, every expression, every gesture. For Mary, everything else in the house seemed to disappear.

From the kitchen, Martha could hear the muffled voices in the other room rise and fall as her company talked and laughed together. Jesus had a kind voice. She wondered what they were talking about. But the more she listened, the more impatient she grew that Mary was relaxing in the other room while she did all the work. Didn't she know how much food had to be prepared? Didn't she know how important this meal was? Didn't she understand that she should be *helping*?

Finally, when Martha could stand it no longer, she marched into the living room and, filled with indignation, said to Jesus, "Lord, don't you care that my sister has left me to do the work by myself? Tell her to help me!" (Luke 10:40)

Pretty bold move, actually. I wonder if an awkward hush hung in the room for a few long seconds while everyone waited for Jesus' response.

"Martha, Martha," the Lord answered, "you are worried and upset about many things, but only one thing
is needed. Mary has chosen what is better, and it will
not be taken away from her" (Luke 10:41-42).

These two verses are very important because they are the
foundation for the rest of this book, so I want to make a couple
of key observations. Let me start by giving you two other trans-
lations:

The Master said, "Martha, dear Martha, you're fussing far too much and getting yourself worked up
over nothing. One thing only is essential, and Mary
has chosen it—it's the main course, and won't be
taken from her" (*The Message*).

But the Lord answered her, "Martha, Martha, you
are anxious and troubled about many things, but one
thing is necessary. Mary has chosen the good portion, which will not be taken away from her" (*English Standard Version*).

How Jesus must have loved Martha. I can hear the compassion in his voice as he gently and lovingly tried to help her see
the situation for what it really was. Jesus wasn't rebuking Martha.
He understood all that she was on the inside—hard working,
efficient, proud and determined. Jesus was empathetic; his answer was an invitation…*Come, now. Let go. Sit with your sister Mary
for a while and enjoy my presence. The work will all get done. Come.*

Most Bible scholars agree that in this passage Jesus was
not saying that Martha's work was not important, nor was he

condemning Martha for attending to the meal. Instead he was commending Mary for her choice to sit at his feet and fellowship with him. The situation was not about making a choice between something bad and something good, but rather about the much more difficult place of choosing between two good things, or something good and something *better*. It was a lesson on priorities, and Mary had hers in the right order.

...of all the good "dishes" we have to choose from at life's table, one is better than the rest.

Jesus said only one thing at that moment was "needed, essential, necessary." And he said that Mary had chosen what was "better, the main course, the good portion." Jesus was using a metaphor of the meal they were about to partake—the various dishes on the table—to make a point about spiritual nourishment. Both Martha and Mary were, in their own ways, serving and honoring their Lord, thus being spiritually fed. But Mary had chosen the portion that was *most* nourishing, the *better dish*. Jesus clearly sided with Mary, not because he liked her more or because he wanted to discourage worthwhile activism, but because Martha's busyness was the kind that was unnecessary and led to fussing and finger pointing.

It's easy for us to see in hindsight as we read this passage Martha's error in judgment. The Master teacher, Lord of life, Savior was right in her living room and her attentions were consumed with beans and cornbread! She was so busy trying to *serve* Jesus that she didn't have even a moment to be *with* him. She was passing up the opportunity of a lifetime.

Jesus, however, never passed up the chance to teach those who would hear a lesson from the everyday classroom of life. This snapshot we see out of the scrapbook of Jesus' ministry on earth has one such powerful message—of all the good "dishes" we have to choose from at life's table, one is better than the rest.

As you read through the following pages, I would ask you to keep in your mind the images of the three players in this exchange: Mary sitting attentively at Jesus' feet, Martha, flustered and working in the kitchen, and Jesus' gentle response. I want to use these images to describe two purely hypothetical churches that might exist somewhere today. These churches are fictional composites of bits and pieces of real churches, most of which I have experienced first hand. Any resemblance to your own church is probably accidental.

The Martha Church

The Martha church is a busy place! Everything happens according to a schedule, including the one-hour Sunday morning services, which allot 20 minutes for worship, five for announcements, 30 for the message, and five for the offering and closing prayer.

Much of the facility, including a new multipurpose wing they just built in the hopes of attracting more young couples and families, is well used every day of the week with various meet-

ings, classes, fellowships and activities. English as a Second Language classes and Sign Language classes meet on Mondays. The
gym is used for basketball and volleyball leagues on Tuesday eve-
nings and Saturdays. On Wednesday mornings, the women's group
has a Bible study and the evening is filled with all-church activities. A scouting troop meets in the fellowship hall on Thursday,
and on Friday several recovery groups use classrooms. In addition, on any given day, you are likely to find other things going on
that range from political interest gatherings to special seminars.
The pastor and staff hope that many who use the building for
these kinds of activities will consider making it their church home.
It is no wonder that the Martha church pastor sometimes feels
more like an activities director than a spiritual shepherd.

In addition to being busy, the Martha church is a very
friendly place with lots of opportunities to socialize. Fellowship
is big here, and comes in all shapes and sizes. There's a place for
everyone to belong—singles, seniors, young married couples,
empty-nesters, widows and divorcees. And if you are recovering
from an addiction, have had an abortion, have lost a loved one,
are unemployed, or have been abused, there are special meetings
you can attend to find comfort through interaction with others
who have gone through similar experiences. Every peg has a hole,
and every hole has a peg. After all, Martha's in charge.

With so many things going on, service is highly regarded
and applauded. The more a person does in and for the church,
the more esteemed he or she becomes. The walls are dotted with
plaques of achievement and most pieces of furniture are dedi-

cated to "Marthas" who gave generously of their time and resources. The church is driven by a well-articulated, goal-oriented statement of purpose that is displayed prominently in the foyer.

Programs in the Martha church are certainly not accidental or random. They are the products of demographic studies and research that assess the makeup of the community. The church planners strive to hone in on specific needs and wants and then design activities to meet those needs in order to draw people in. The messages, too, are tailored to the perceived desires of the population. You are likely to hear sermons at the Martha church that have a very practical, culturally relevant flair such as "Seven Habits of Highly Effective Families," "Godly Principles for Business Success," or "Bible Heroes Character Series...Lessons for Today."

People are at the very heart of the Martha church, so every effort is made to make them feel welcomed, comfortable and engaged. To that end, the landscaping is immaculate and there are plenty of visitors' parking spots in front. The services are fast-moving and entertaining, relying on techniques such as multi-screen projection systems, high tech video shows, drama, celebrity appearances or Broadway quality musical performances to keep people interested and ensure their return. Numerical growth is the primary measuring stick for the church's health or success, so the leaders are constantly searching for that perfect combination of ingredients that makes a good impression on visitors while keeping current members happy and committed.

Since image is important to Martha, the church is constantly striving toward state of the art youth and children's facilities with the latest trendy components—cafés, game rooms, computers, recreation areas and my favorite, coffee shops (extra hot latte, light vanilla please!). The children's and youth ministries are high priority because the pastor says, "If we can reach the kids, the parents will follow." He's willing to spend money on whatever will bring in more tithers, because he's deep in debt from the current building and is already under pressure to add more space.

The Sunday morning routine provides plenty of time and space for people to visit in a relaxed atmosphere because personal interaction is a high priority. Greeters are at every door and the coffee and donuts are fresh. In order to maintain the upbeat, dynamic image during the services, the pastoral staff steers clear of anything that might become emotional or upsetting to visitors. The praise and worship time is intellectual and metered. The pastor keeps a tight reign on order and both eyes on the clock. The people in the seats tend more toward spectators than participants, and consumers than worshipers.

Follow-up in the Martha church happens like clockwork. Visitor letters go out Monday afternoon and personal calls or visits may be made to particularly distinguished or influential prospective members. The sermon topics are always set at least three months ahead so that advertising postcards can be mass mailed each quarter. With so many churches in the area, the leaders devote a good portion of the church's budget to first class marketing. They worry that if they don't get the word out about all they have to offer, someone else will end up with their share of the church seeking "pie."

The Martha church, like the woman, loves Jesus and works hard to please him. A beautiful artist's rendition of him surrounded by children hangs in the church foyer right next to the pastor's picture. The pastor just finished a sermon series outlining the historical evidence of the resurrection, and the education department offers a Sunday school class about his life and miracles. Every Easter they do a pageant, and every Christmas a live nativity scene along with an elaborate light display, all of which, they are proud to note, are well-attended by many in the community who attend other churches or don't have a church home at all.

They worry that if they don't get the word out about all they have to offer, someone else will end up with their share of the church seeking "pie."

Jesus in the Martha church is savior, comforter, provider and healer. He is the one in whom you have the promise of heaven and the one who can help you when life is more than you can handle. Faithful and loving, he is always there to pick you up when you fall short. He is full of forgiveness and mercy. The people desire his blessing on their lives and express their love to him through holiness and service. They strive to be true followers and representatives of Christ, studying his examples and living out his teachings. The youth sell trendy "Jesus" t-shirts and are bold in proclaiming their faith at school and in the community.

The church wants to be known in the community as one that teaches the Bible, spiritual living and a better way in Christ. Their theology is sound without extremes. They have a discipleship program, several intense Biblical study classes, an apologetics course and a missions training school. The congregation is made up of families and individuals sincere in their desire to pass on their Christian heritage to the next generation and live godly lives. Many parents in the church will admit that one of the main reasons they attend is for their kids. They know what's out there, and they see the church environment as a safe haven that can hopefully steer their children in the right direction, while somehow shielding them from harmful influences.

The Martha church desires to pray, but it seems to have a hard time sustaining prayer efforts long term. They do, however, have a prayer chain that has been in place for several years. Anyone who needs prayer can initiate the chain by calling Martha, a widow who has been in charge of the group for two years. She struggles sometimes to keep enough names on the list to handle all the requests, but she knows it is worth the effort. People just seem to lose interest after a while, and the rate of attrition is discouraging. She doesn't understand why people start with such enthusiasm to pray, but don't stay committed. Lately they have been so overwhelmed with many in their church who are battling serious illnesses that she is going to meet with the pastor to hopefully figure out a way to recruit some fresh faces.

Occasionally, the pastor will call for a prayer vigil when they have a particularly large financial need or when they are facing a crisis. Just last year, for example, the building fund came up short at a crucial time because monies promised were not coming in as expected. The contractor in charge of the new addition threatened to back out with the work only partly completed. So the church had a Saturday afternoon prayer vigil. They needed a large donation to get things back on track. Sure enough, the following week, one of the church members came forward with a special contribution that was enough to keep the contractor on the job and the completion date on schedule. They firmly believe that prayer is the answer to life's difficulties and that God will come through with a solution if they pray hard enough.

The Martha church also advocates the importance of reaching out to the community through a variety of charitable ministries, which are coordinated by the evangelism minister. They support a food pantry and a mentoring program for troubled teens. They also sponsor girls' and boys' scouting troops, and a meals-on-wheels program for shut-ins. They have a passion to serve and take pride in all they do to care for the homeless and poor.

However, the evangelism minister's big event each year is the annual month long "Focus on Evangelism" campaign during which everyone is encouraged to share their faith and bring friends to church. It is, in effect, a membership drive that usually nets 25% to 30% of their average annual growth. Because of how active and visible the church is in the community, it attracts a few new families each month who are drawn by the program opportunities and energy. Ninety-five percent of their new members each year say they join because they are simply "looking for more" from a church.

The Martha Pastor

The Martha church pastor is 43 years old with a wife and three children. He is always on the go. His cell phone number is in the church bulletin because he wants his congregation to feel he's accessible. He's always on call when someone has a crisis, even in the middle of the night. He will leave his lawn half mowed or excuse himself from a family cookout because Martha's mother has been taken to the hospital and wants him there to comfort her family. He does pastoral counseling for free.

He delivers food, picks up city kids for Wednesday night youth activities, and drives Martha to the cemetery on the other side of town once a month to put flowers on her husband's grave. (They've been members of the church for 25 years, and he served on the board of trustees for ten.) When conflict arises, he puts on his striped shirt and mediates the problem away. He has learned how to patiently hear out the opinions and ideas of other people, while guarding his own.

The Martha pastor can even do small plumbing jobs—that's how he worked his way through seminary. While on visitation, he listens intently to tangled webs of family prayer needs (gossip) and enthusiastically admires handmade quilts, wedding photos and ceramic bird collections. He always accepts a piece of pie with his coffee, even if he'd rather not, because it's a family recipe. And with all the money that comes in from the annual fundraising bake sale, he sees it as an investment.

Once a week, Pastor has lunch with one of his staff members so he can stay involved in their lives and encourage them in ministry. He listens to their prayer requests and prays faithfully for each one in his personal devotion time. As a show of support, he tries to drop in on several of the numerous activities that go on at the church during the week, including various committee meetings, because he knows people like to see him around. He even sits in the dunking booth every year at the fall festival. He's a big hit.

The Martha pastor likes to have his personal prayer and study time in the morning when he's not at an early pastors' breakfast, men's meeting, or out on call. He wants to be diligent and give his people fresh words every Sunday, but his preparation time seems to be inadequate and is often interrupted. He sees preaching as the most important thing he does and the reason he gets paid. He also knows it is the most important criteria in determining the length of his tenure as senior pastor. Carrying the torch of a long line of great orators in his pulpit, he feels pressured to do it well because his people expect it. Sometimes, when he's in a pinch, he turns to the internet for good sermons written by great men and women of God. He figures no one really cares where they come from, and quite honestly, they go over pretty well.

He feels guilty when he's not at the office during the week, however it's rare that he has any quiet time when he's there because of the steady stream of phone calls and visitors that comes in for him. The pace keeps him feeling tired and spiritually cheated—his cup is running dry. He wishes he could figure out how to slow down, but he's afraid to ask for time away. Who would keep all the plates spinning? If he draws apart for too long, people start asking questions. He bears the burden of being indispensable, and yet thrives on the notion at the same time.

> *He bears the burden of being "indispensable," and yet thrives on the notion at the same time.*

The pastor's schedule takes a toll on his family too. His kids wonder why he's so warm and friendly at church, and so grumpy when he gets home. His wife has become his sounding board and she secretly resents the church for intruding so much into their daily lives. But she understands that her presence is important as well, so she sits in the front row every Sunday, teaches Sunday school and attends the women's Bible study meetings during the week. While she wishes things were a little different, she figures the next church would be the same, and the salary package and retirement plan give her a sense of stability and security.

When he's not being "available," the Martha pastor works hard to stay informed on current technology and church trends. His bookshelves are full of church growth theories, research, and

successful church profiles. He attends seminars on the weekends
when he can, but is always sure to be back in the pulpit Sunday
morning. Many people in the church simply won't stay to hear a
guest preacher, and the offering suffers.

As the image sustainer, he also extends himself out into
the community every opportunity he gets. In addition to pastors'
functions, he is involved with two different business groups that
meet monthly for networking. One is a Christian businessmen's
group; the other is a think tank made up of many of the most
prominent people in the community including the mayor, some
city council men and women, several doctors and attorneys, a
few professors from the local college, and two local television
personalities.

He's learned a lot from these two groups. In fact, he sees
himself as a CEO of sorts, and has applied much of what he's
learned about the business world to leading his church. Many of
the same principles are at work—supply and demand, the customer is always right, target marketing and image management.
He's as good as any corporate executive at managing people, time
and resources.

Although the Martha pastor entered into the ministry with
his eyes on Jesus and a passion to preach conviction and salvation, his years in church leadership have caused him to rely more
and more on his experience and knowledge base. Much of the
energy he used to put into personal prayer and worship, he now
spends on books, video sets and other training materials that
promise the keys to a successful church. Where he once was in-

novative and bold, now he's more reluctant to take risks or push change because it's often not worth the punishment. He has a few scars to prove it.

The last really creative idea he had was an alternative Saturday night service to reach a counterculture audience, but by the time the proposal made it through several committees, it had been whittled down to something unrecognizable and he was getting hate mail from a handful of strong opponents. He decided the price tag was just too high and he let it go.

Sometimes he wonders why he's so tired, and he wonders about stories he hears of great revivals and awakenings in other churches. But the truth is he's confident in his ability to figure out what the people want and then deliver. The money is flowing, his facility is better than average, his people are active and happy, new families continue to trickle in, and he feels the church is doing some good things in the area. With things going so well, he reasons, why tinker with success?

That's what the Martha church looks like, and it's a fairly familiar scene. Sincere, devoted Christians, under the leadership of an ambitious, entrepreneurial pastor, serving each other and the community with their combined resources and talents. It's not a bad thing. However, in the next chapter, let's look a little deeper into this picture at some of the dynamics that are at work.

Discussion Questions

1. In Luke 10:41-42, was Jesus condemning Martha's actions? Do you think Jesus appreciated being served in the manner Martha was serving?

2. The Bible doesn't tell us whether Martha ever came and sat with her sister, or whether she kept working. What do you think?

3. Share a time when you felt "stuck in the kitchen." Compare your attitude to Martha's.

4. What makes the Martha church tick? How does it define success?

5. Why do you think this church struggles to maintain prayer? List several ideas.

6. What would be the most difficult thing about pastoring the Martha church? How could the congregation help?

THE CONSUMER BASED CHURCH

The Martha church is actually what I call a consumer based church, a church driven and shaped primarily by the needs of its market. It is pushed and pulled in every direction according to what the "customer" says it will take to make him happy. It has adopted the world's system of consumerism and all the tenets thereof. You might say they live in the book of Numbers.

In Sally Morgenthaler's book *Worship Evangelism*, Elmer Towns describes the consumer based church phenomenon:

> America's Protestants choose churches on the basis
> of what affirms us, entertains us, satisfies us or makes
> us feel good about God and ourselves. If we recog-
> nize church worshipers as consumers, we will recog-

nize church programs as menus, and types of worship as the main entrees in the restaurant.... [C]onsumers go where the menus fit their taste.... [T]he church menus Americans seek are not filled with doctrinal options but with a variety of worship options. Americans go where they feel comfortable with the style of worship that best reflects their inclinations and temperament.[1]

Sally adds:

Consequently, congregations like Anywhere Community Church go into hyperspeed, honing a worship style that is sure to appeal to society's self-oriented tastes. Worship packaging (the image, the sound, the delivery) becomes everything, while the stuff of worship (what Jesus called "spirit and truth" in John 4:24) becomes a memory.[2]

Consumerism has dominated our culture since the industrial revolution when the days of self-sufficient households ended. The department store replaced the loom and the grocery store replaced the family farm. Independence was sold to the Nasdaq as we became totally dependent on manufacturers to produce and sell the things we needed and wanted. Suddenly every person who could spend a nickel became a potential customer, and the competition between retailers for market domination began. Fickle, demanding and highly sought after, the individual consumer was the prize.

The consumer driven marketplace feeds on such factors as

ingenuity, entertainment, location and image. The mottos are "Make the customer happy...very happy. Give them what they want and they will come back for more. Make a profit at all cost."

Consumerism is important to the economic balance. It plays a significant role in the supply and demand equation that keeps the availability and price of goods and services in healthy proportion. However, it also creates an environment in which only the strongest "suppliers" survive. Only those retailers that can give us the most for our money stay in business. Every CEO knows, get a little behind the times, and you're history. Just ask Kmart and Montgomery Ward. Ask any downtown general store—if you can find one still open—that's done battle with Wal-Mart. Consumerism leaves in its wake those who can't give us more for less, faster and with a smile.

While consumerism has its place in the marketplace, it's not hard to see why it becomes a toxic virus when it is allowed to bleed over into the church world. When a church buys into the consumerism model, it begins to look more like a country club or a business on Main Street than a part of Jesus' bride.

They ask the same questions: What do people want? Are they lonely? Do they have children? What are their fears and concerns? Do they lack meaning in life? Are they more interested in spirituality or practicality? Should we rename sin and call it dysfunction? What kind of music do they like? The whole thing becomes a people to people affair based on research and statistics. They do religious things based on careful assessment of human behavior in the "church industry."

Cultural Relevance

One of the buzz phrases in consumer based churches is "cultural relevance." Those churches that market to people to fill the building all chase the current trends and spend a lot of energy trying to figure out what appeals to each generation and how to incorporate it. The epitome of the "cultural relevance" mentality is this suggestion made by one very highly respected church consulting team—if you want to evaluate the effectiveness of a worship service to reach people today, videotape it and then play it back side-by-side with a television tuned to MTV. The more similarity there is, the more likely that the service will communicate the gospel to people, especially those under 40. They also recommend that churches eliminate any period of silence during worship that lasts longer than five seconds![2]

...being culturally relevant in a melting pot society that encompasses many generations is a complicated task.

That blew me away when I first read it. The problem is that being culturally relevant in a melting pot society that encompasses many generations is a complicated task. George Barna identified five age groups or generations of Americans: Seniors (born 1926 and earlier), Builders (born 1927-1945), Boomers (born 1946-1964), Busters (born 1965-1983), and Mosaics (born 1984-present).[4] Each of these subsets has different priorities, different world views, and different perceived spiritual needs. Throw in a wide variety of ethnic and socioeconomic groups that comprise our nation, and you begin to get the picture. Each sector looks for something slightly different in a church, which makes true cultural relevance a totally relative and practically impossible goal for churches to achieve!

Pastor Dan Scott hammers the idea of relevance in his book *The Emerging American Church*. A Pentecostal by upbringing and a traditionalist that defends the catholicity—the ageless disciplines, doctrines and traditions—of Christianity, he paints a starkly pathetic picture of church leaders lost in their effort to package church for public acceptance:

> …[T]he goddess of relevance, whom we Americans serve with unceasing high and reverent honors, changes her mind almost daily. She is a fickle and [spiteful] goddess. Those who serve her cannot find her, even in the day they seek her with all of their hearts.

> The elders of many of the great denominations have rushed to the temple of relevance to worship her over the cries of their own parishioners. These church leaders have no idea how ridiculous they have become, even in the eyes of the pagans and the godless. They seem unaware, bowing to the goddess, that she laughs as their calamity comes.

> The joke is cruel: The bowing elders are, horror of horrors, irrelevant. Why? Because the masses of

American Christians, the same Christians that the
elders were supposed to be leading to a relevant faith,
are actually seeking the ancient faith, the same faith
the elders abandoned in favor of progress![5]

I don't know that I could defend the line that Dan drew in
the sand, because anyone who knows me knows that I am all for
creativity in ministry! The church I started and pastored for 16
years was much more likely to be described as "contemporary"
than "traditional." However, there is a big difference between a
church embracing the new things God is doing, and trying to
incorporate every new trend and fad that sweeps through secular
society. Being *relevant* to the culture is not necessarily the same as
being *like* it. As George Barna wisely concludes, "We must be
careful to adapt to our environment in ways that establish the
relevance of Christianity without going overboard in our efforts
to accommodate people's needs and desires."[6]

Sheep Shifting

The goal of the consumer based church is to get more
people, and therefore all of its energy is given toward attracting
new members and keeping the current ones in place. Unfortunately, when the objective is to fill the building with people, no
one really stops to ask or care where the people are coming from.
"Transfer growth"—accepting members who wish to transfer
from another church—is completely acceptable and goes unques-
tioned. It all too often replaces true evangelism and conversion
growth—increasing membership by actually winning lost people
to Jesus who previously had no church home.

I call this process "shifting sheep," and it is the tragic explanation behind the fact that while some churches in America
appear to be growing exponentially, Christianity as a whole is
basically stagnant. The Barna Research Group states that despite
churches having raised and spent more than $500 billion dollars
in the past decade to try and influence America's spiritual life, the
percentage of adults who attend church in a typical week has
changed little over the past five years, fluctuating between 40%
and 43%.[7] The number of adults who call themselves born again
Christians has also changed very little in the same time period,
ranging between 38% and 41%.[8] In other words, very few churches
are producing new converts—we are just redistributing the flock.

William Chadwick, in his book *Stealing Sheep: The Church's
Hidden Problem with Transfer Growth*, explains the scenario this way:

> Today we have moving church bodies filled with
> church shoppers and ecclesiastical consumers, join-
> ing churches for personal gain and leaving them for
> the same reason.
>
> The McChurch has replaced the traditional home
> church and its relational values. Fast-food Christians
> pull up to ecclesiastical drive-through windows, or-
> der their McGroups, consume the experience and
> then drive off, discarding relationships like burger
> wrappers on the highway of life. Savvy church
> growth pastors quickly learned that significant growth
> can occur if a church learns how to market its burgers
> to capture the appetite of this roving crowd.[9]

You don't have to think too hard about the concept of sheep shifting to understand why consumerism in the church world breeds serious levels of competition between congregations. Churches that should and could be working together to further the gospel in their city are instead locked in marketing battles fighting over who gets the Smiths and the Joneses. Storefront churches and mega churches flourish at the expense of the older or smaller mainline churches, even to the point of death, without a bit of remorse. Few are thinking about how to win their city for Christ because they're too busy trying to figure out how to herd more sheep into their own shed.

In a community I have visited on several occasions, two very large churches are locked in a marketing battle to be top dog. Their battlefield is the family mailbox. One Easter one of the churches sent out a big postcard advertising 40,000 eggs at their Easter egg hunt. Within days, the other sent a slick flyer boasting 50,000 eggs at their Easter egg hunt, adding that it was the largest in the state. Six months later, when both churches were—quite coincidentally, I'm sure—building new multi-million dollar facilities, two more advertisements went out. The first church proudly announced

> *Few are thinking about how to win their city for Christ because they're too busy trying to figure out how to herd more sheep into their own shed.*

that its new children's building was being painted by a former Disney graphic artist. The second church rebutted with a children's building decorated in an undersea adventure theme.

The sad thing is, marketing plastic candy-filled eggs and painted walls works! In fact, in the family community served by these two churches, it works incredibly well. The gospel is for sale and when they creatively and culturally customize it, they can attract the masses. They've done their homework and they know what the triple-digit income, SUV driving suburban families want. These consumers expect excellence in everything from the schools to the public services—churches included. They will go where the deals seem the sweetest until something makes them angry or a better offer comes along. Loyalty is a mirage in the consumer based church because the customer holds the cards.

While some sheep stealing is overt and intentional, much of it happens because church leaders simply look the other way, choosing not to question or jeopardize growth they may be experiencing. The reasoning goes like this: "We're not really *trying* to take members from other churches; they're just coming because of the great things going on here. What's wrong with that? Besides, it's their right to choose, and there's really nothing we can do about it."

William Chadwick himself admits to turning a blind eye to transfer growth as a pastor:

> Sheep stealing appealed greatly to my need to provide for, feed and please people. The tattered and disenchanted newcomers, turned on by our worship

experience, elicited in me the same emotions that I used to have for a stray dog or cat that showed up at our farmhouse in Vermont. First you feed them, then you begin liking them, and soon you name them and refer to them as your own.[10]

Unfortunately, sheep shifting has become an accepted way to grow a church and has been defended by church growth consultants who say that people have the right to leave a church if it is not meeting their spiritual needs. While this line of thinking is hard to argue with, particularly in our consumer mentality, it is not very New Testament. Chadwick explains why:

> Transfer growth, by definition, creates no numerical growth in the kingdom of God. In fact the term is an oxymoron, and grossly misleading, for its net result is simply much ado about nothing. There are no new converts, no baptisms, no expansion of knowledge of God in the world, and no salvation fruit from this labor. Arguably—and contrary to popular belief—there is no known purely positive kingdom benefit from a membership change.[11]

The price of sheep stealing is huge. True evangelism suffers due to a false impression of church growth. Competition between churches turns nasty and leaves behind too many casualties, fostering resentment that kills any hope of cooperation. Most importantly though, disgruntled church members move from one congregation to another, spreading the viruses of accusation, bitterness and unforgivness. The entire body of Christ suffers when consumer based churches abort the Great Commission to feed their own ambitions.

The Problem with Vanity

Since image is critical to the consumer based church, time and energy are often wasted on things of little or no importance. For example, the pastor keeps a new pair of shoes in his office that are designated as "pulpit shoes," not to be worn anywhere else. Before every service, he changes into the new shoes so that when he sits in the pulpit chair on the platform during the service, the soles of his feet do not appear scuffed or worn. Or, when image is important, a church finds itself in a bitter dispute over whether to put pews or chairs in the new sanctuary because that decision greatly affects how others view it. They might even add or take away chairs in the sanctuary as the attendance fluctuates so the room always looks full. When image matters, more money than necessary may go into cathedral ceilings inlaid with gold, over-the-top projection systems and executive style salary packages. The problem with vanity is that it can cause a church to major in minors while really significant matters go unattended.

And with the church bustling with activity, overlooking the obvious can be easy. Busy-ness effectively hides the lack of spiritual substance and depth. If everyone is involved and things are stirring, the reasoning goes, then we must be getting somewhere. But where?

While all the activities at the Martha church serve a worthwhile purpose and can be very helpful, if they fail to bring people into an encounter with the living God, and not just other people, then someone needs to ask the tough question: Are they really part of a kingdom agenda? Serving others is good and there is certainly nothing wrong with working hard, unless of course it causes you to completely ignore the fact that Jesus is in the other room.

Sally Morgenthaler says that even boomers and busters, to whom "seeker friendly" churches market, are leaving those churches because they came searching for spiritual substance and they found something that looked too much like the business world that they live in every day—professional presentations, sharp dressed managers and a sales pitch illustrated with a Power Point slideshow. She asserts that people really don't want church to look just like the world. They get enough performance based achievement on the job. When they come to church, they want something different; they want a personal encounter with the living God.[12]

The Team Mascot - Jesus

While God is proclaimed in the Martha church, his role is often relegated to helping the people and meeting their needs as they see fit. He is God made in man's image, restricted to exist and act within their theological box. Jesus, likewise, is part of the church community, but he is treated somewhat as an historical figure—the founder of the movement and chief source for help when human resources fail. You can go to Sunday morning services week after week and never hear his name mentioned once.

As David Bryant suggests, Jesus is not the *master*, but the *mascot* that cheers from the sidelines while the real team carries out the plays. He is in the background, incidental to the main event.

My daughter used to be the mascot for her high school football team, the A&M Consolidated Tigers. We kept the tiger suit hanging in the hall closet. For some reason, that's what I thought of when I saw this perplexing sign on a church message board, "Have you seen *our* Jesus?" as if he were the team tiger. It made me wonder how their Jesus differed from the one the rest of us are familiar with. And I wondered how Jesus felt about being *theirs*. How careless and arrogant to think that we could own the Son of God or try him out like a new truck model!

> *Jesus is not the master, but the mascot that cheers from the sidelines while the real team carries out the plays.*

In the consumer based church, Jesus is a beloved figure, but the reality is that he plays second fiddle to the personalities of key people. The Martha church is personality sustained. While it can be driven by the personality of a particularly high profile lay person, typically it is the pastor's personality that takes center stage. He or she becomes the dominant focal point and the defining element for the church's identity. Just look at the Religion section of your local newspaper—it looks like a personality contest.

The pastor's name is on the church sign, in the phone book listing, and on the church letterhead. His picture appears on the Sunday bulletin and is always on advertising pieces that go out to the community. His image and identity are so intertwined with the church's that they are really one in the same. If you didn't know any better, to look at their literature, you would have to conclude that he is the church, and the church is he.

One of my pet peeves is the trend among local church clergy and other independent ministers of the gospel to give themselves titles such as "Apostle," or "Bishop" and then insist that everyone address them in that manner. I'm not talking about organizational or denominational titles given as part of a system of identification for leaders in their own ranks. That's a sacred cow I'll leave alone, at least in this book. I'm referring to the self-appointment of such titles by lone rangers who just want recognition and are using their platform to get it. There is no room in the gospel message for self-importance or promotion. Jesus can't be preeminent when people and personalities are on top and out in front.

With adoration and attention focused on a person or people, Jesus is easily ignored or taken advantage of. The consumer based church can have meetings, teach classes, answer phones, raise money, feed the poor, sing songs and even do services without thinking much at all about Jesus. When things are clicking along, they really don't need him. Educated, independent, resourceful people can do a lot for each other with their own abilities, making it difficult for them to feel dependent on anyone, even God.

Prayer and the Cosmic Genie

I preached once in a large downtown church whose services were televised locally. We met behind the stage before the service—primarily for my benefit as the visitor—to go over the schedule, which was detailed down to the second. They did this every week and had worked it down to a science. Everyone knew where they were supposed to stand and precisely how long each segment of the program was to last.

As we were about to make our entrance, I asked, "Could we pray before we go in?" I might as well have lit a cigarette. They were embarrassed and flustered. The senior pastor did his best to utter a perfunctory prayer, despite his obvious concern that it might put us a few seconds behind in the telecast schedule.

Sally Morgenthaler's candid observation is true:

Too often we worship our methodologies while feigning devotion to God. And when we do this, our pride and self-reliance belie a humanism more secular and infinitely more grotesque than anything we abhor in the world.[13]

This kind of "Christian humanism"—serving God based on the resources of people—is why the prayer life of the consumer based church is stalled in crisis mode. They believe in prayer, but treat it as a bail bonding service. Only when people don't come through with a solution do they turn to God. They pray primarily when they are backed into a corner, and then they expect God to perform. But with money in the bank, a good location and a clever strategy, they don't really need him otherwise.

Problematic prayer is anemic and dangerous. While God does love to meet our needs, he is not a cosmic genie. If we only relate to him when we have a problem that needs solving, we are setting ourselves up for some big disappointments. When God doesn't perform to our liking, disillusionment and doubt can swoop in because there is no real substance to our relationship with him. We don't know how to wait or worship; we don't know what it means to hunger or seek. All we know is how to ask.

I sat next to a man on an airplane not too long ago who happened to be a member of the church I was going to visit in Georgia. He and his wife had been faithful members there for more than 20 years, teaching Sunday school and serving on several committees. Several months earlier, his wife had been diagnosed with cancer and the church rallied around them in prayer for healing. However, her last checkup at the doctor revealed a discouraging prognosis—the cancer was spreading rapidly.

The man was hurt and angry, both at his church and at God. He felt let down and betrayed. All he had ever understood about God was in question because the sales pitch he bought into when he signed on wasn't holding up. He expected pie in the sky and on his personal table as well, a theology that was now begging for a deeper explanation.

Who's in Charge Here?

All churches are defined by one central issue—control. An institution sold out to people is going to get only what people can offer. In the consumer based church, everything is about people. Minister to the people. Fill the building with people. Meet the needs of the people. Convince the people to give. At the end of the game, he who has the most people wins.

The problem is that when we sell church to the people, they own it. It becomes *their* sanctuary, *their* program, *their* pew, *their* building. The more they invest, the more ownership they feel. Furthermore, what people own, they feel entitled to control. *"I built this church with my own sweat and tears. Why won't you hire my wife?" "I gave $20,000 for a baby grand piano. Why does the worship committee want an organ overhaul instead?" "I've poured hours of work into this program and we've been doing it for years. What do you mean it's time for a change?"* When the sheep take over the shed, the church will find itself choking on the inside from opinions run amuck.

The need to be in control stems from all kinds of insecurities and fears. Maintain the institution, sustain the image, and keep the boat steady so everything feels the same week after week. It's natural to resist change because change makes us feel vulnerable and unsure. And when the enemy finds a church in which people are vying for control, he can really work havoc.

I was in an old Pennsylvania church doing a prayer conference several years ago, and I stepped out the back door of the building during a break for some fresh air. There, about 20 yards away, sat a beautiful new sanctuary (the building we were in was fairly old and musty). I asked the pastor what the story was, and this is what he told me:

Last year the people voted to build a new sanctuary.

We quickly raised the money for it, hired the contractors, broke ground and watched as it went up. It was exciting! I thought God was really doing something. But when the project was completed and it came time to move into the new building, the old-timers wouldn't budge. "Too many memories in this old sanctuary," they said. I've done everything I know to do, but they just won't leave. It caused a huge split in the congregation and almost cost me my job.

The "controlites" in a consumer based church can be anywhere—in the committee system, the choir, on the pastoral staff or in the pews. They can be denominational hierarchy, the money holders, or tenured members who have seen pastors come and go. They can be large in number or very few. Even one or two can have a detrimental impact.

A friend of mine attends a church in Florida where the pastor has a heart and passion for worship, prayer and community transformation. The church has a "prayer room" that he agrees could be a center for strategic, informed prayer for their missionaries, the city, the lost, even global concerns. But he has one problem. The designated room was furnished by a woman in memory of her deceased husband, and therefore the pastor is afraid to alter it in any way. As a result, the room stands basically unused, except as a sitting room furnished with several chairs and wall hangings. It is, in reality, a shrine to the man, complete with a plaque on the door bearing his name.

Church "plaque" is worse than tooth decay. It builds up in

the system and constricts the flow of life-giving moves of the Spirit. Older churches with a long history of "plaque-itis" can literally become dysfunctional and weak from the disease.

The reason is simple: Every plaque you see in a church marks a piece of furniture or structure that can never be moved, altered or discarded (Oh! The very idea!) until the donor and all of his or her descendents graduate from this life or leave the church. Regardless of what is inscribed on the front, the fine print on the back, which many pastors don't see until it's too late, says, "*Mine!* Don't touch!"

Church "plaque" is worse than tooth decay.

Controlites' attacks can be noticeable or subtle, but are always very literal and damaging. They steal ideas, visions and dreams, and are like cold molasses on the process of change. They can be downright vicious when someone tries to change *their* church. I have seen sweet, gray-haired ladies grow fangs and blow fire because the pastor allowed a synthesizer into *their* sanctuary or turned *their* parlor into a bookstore.

Since the consumer based church generally moves by vote and consensus, someone is always unhappy. Martha doesn't take it very well when things don't go her way. When she loses, everyone loses because she'll vote again and again with her face, her finances and her feet. She may leave the church, or simply hold a "parking lot committee" meeting to undermine any progress that she opposes. I have seen it over and over.

In a traditional Michigan church where I was honored to be a guest preacher one Sunday morning, I noticed that the organist was crocheting and reading a magazine while I spoke, all while still seated in the front of the sanctuary at the organ. After the service, I asked the pastor about it. He told me that they had recently introduced some new, more contemporary praise music in addition to hymns, and she didn't like it. To add insult to injury, the new projection screen covered up the organ pipes. So she was casting her vote in a very visible, distracting way every Sunday! I actually had a lady in one of my first churches as a young preacher that would stick her fingers in her ears when I preached certain messages that she didn't think were "Methodist" enough!

Another great example of a control battle came from a church in Arkansas where I spoke. I noticed that all the people seated on one side of the sanctuary seemed fairly interested, while the people seated on the other side of the sanctuary looked like they had been eating sour pickles. Again, I asked the pastor what was going on, and he explained that they had recently put new carpet in the building, and that the "sour pickle" group lost the vote. They wanted blue but the majority had voted for green.

Even a pastor can become a controller. In a large Chicago church one Sunday morning, the pastor, who had come under fire recently for some changes he wanted to make, invited everyone who disagreed with him to stand. Then he invited all those who were standing to leave! He literally asked the ushers to open the back doors, and escort the dissenters out.

Pastor Fetch

Typically, though, the pastor is on the receiving end of control issues. The Martha pastor, who works so hard to be available to people and keep up with trends, can be nicknamed "Pastor Fetch" because someone is always yanking on his leash. Just whistle and he'll be there. He is a servant of the people and the keeper of the image. His primary job, whether it is stated or not, is to keep the people happy.

Pastor Fetch is at high risk of becoming a casualty in the consumer based church. While it feels good to be needed by so many people at first, it eventually becomes a burden too heavy to carry. Pastor Fetch quickly learns that it is impossible to make everyone happy at the same time, and impossible to make some people happy at all. He learns that he can never be available enough, even though he's available 24 hours a day, and that letters marked "personal" always start with, "Pastor, we love you, but…."

He also discovers that no matter how "on top of things" he stays, he can never rest because to be on the cutting edge means to be changing and creating all the time. He feels the other churches nipping at his heels and he has to come up with another program, a more dynamic service, and newer, bigger, better stuff to keep the people from shopping elsewhere. Blue-light specials, pies for visitors, balloons for children, big name endorsements, special events, more landscaping—his head spins when he lies down at night and asks himself in the words of Christopher Robins, "*Now, how to amuse them today?*"[14]

I stood in the dark hall of a church in New York, where the seasoned pastor had been brought in to pull the church out of a nosedive. At 57 years old, he had invested for three tough years the energy of a man half his age with remarkable results noted throughout the area. He had spent himself there, and was seeing his effort pay off as the church stabilized and had begun to grow under his committed, spiritual leadership.

Right before I arrived, however, he had received a lunch invitation from some of the long standing members of the congregation. They had thanked him for all his hard work, and concluded by saying, "We really appreciate all you've done, but we think it's time for us to look for a younger pastor now so we can attract more young couples and families. We've already started the process."

That dear pastor cried on my shoulder as he felt the brunt of consumer based thinking. They had gotten from him what they needed, and now they were discarding him like a used up commodity. Loving things and using people is the norm in the consumerism model. Pastors in consumer based churches are sitting ducks for controllers who are used to getting their way, and unless they are rescued, they will eventually die at the hands that feed them.

Summary

We could illustrate the Martha church like this:

Martha Church

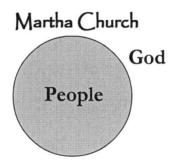

Consumer Based Church

1. Religious Activities

2. Crisis Motivated Prayer

3. Competition

4. Sheep Shifting

5. Jesus as Mascot

6. Pastor Fetch

7. Image Consciousness

8. Personality Driven Leadership

9. Controlites

Too many churches today are in the kitchen with Martha, "worried and distracted about many things." They don't recognize how far off the mark they've grown, because the hum of church machinery and the chorus of opinions has long ago drowned out Jesus' beckoning to come and sit with him. They are so caught up in the work of the Lord, they have no time for the Lord of the work. For so long, they have done church with their own money, education, techniques and experience that they've forgotten his gentle reminder to Martha, "only one thing is needed." *Consumer based churches are not choosing "dishes" that are bad; they are just not choosing the one that is better.*

Discussion Questions

1. Discuss the suggestion on page 36 that church services should resemble MTV if we want them to reach today's "market."

2. What are some of the results of sheep shifting, both for individual churches and the body of Christ as a whole?

3. Discuss church advertising/marketing. Does it work? In what sense? Do you think churches should advertise?

4. How do we treat Jesus like a mascot? How could we treat him more like master?

5. What role does prayer play in the consumer based church?

6. When is activity, even worthwhile activity, not healthy for a church? How much is too much?

7. Why are control struggles so detrimental to a church?

8. Give a brief profile of Pastor Fetch.

THE MARY CHURCH

The Mary church shares many fundamental commonalities with its Martha counterpart. Both face the very real challenges of staffing decisions, financial needs and location logistics such as seating space, parking and building maintenance. Both are comprised of imperfect people who bring to the picture an array of gifts, talents, needs and baggage. Both desire to be a spiritual oasis for their members and a blessing to their communities.

Some of what I will say about the Mary church could also be said about a particular Martha church, just as some of what I said about the Martha church might apply to some Mary churches. That's because it is not just one attribute that defines a church to be one or the other. Churches are complex systems that really have to be experienced in their entirety to be evaluated and understood. The caution is this—don't get too hung up on any one "Martha" or "Mary" characteristic, and certainly don't make judgments about your own church (or anyone else's) based only on one or two points. You can't judge a church by its exterior any more than you can judge a book by its cover.

Keep in mind that I said these descriptions are "fictional composites"—characterizations based on real churches, but not representing any one actual church. Like a caricature, they unequally depict the most prominent features; therefore, they are meant to be read as examples, not hard and fast prototypes. Focus on the principles and the big picture. Furthermore, while I am presenting both the Martha and the Mary churches as moderately sized because it gives me more descriptive latitude, either can be very large or very small. Both can present themselves in infinite ways according to the culture and community they serve.

That being said, there is something different about the Mary church. It is a unique place where creativity abounds. People often describe it as…well, different. It can be hard to put a finger on exactly what it is, but you *feel* it when you're there.

One of the first things one might notice on Sunday morning in the Mary church is a distinctively different worship atmosphere. One of the key differences is what I would describe as relaxed flexibility. Though there is a relatively traditional order to the service, it does not click along with stopwatch precision. Instead, it flows with some freedom to linger or move on as the worship experience unfolds. An impromptu testimony, a song that wasn't planned, a special time of prayer for an urgent need—these types of "interruptions" are common and don't create anxiety or tension. The services are a unique combination of Spirit-sensitive planning and well-managed unpredictability.

Worship and personal prayer ministry dominate a large part of the service, especially the first half, and housecleaning details such as announcements are saved for last. In addition, rather than using the corporate worship time to cover a long list of church business, new classes, upcoming events or financial reports, this information is printed and made available in the bulletin and in the foyer for people to read on their own.

The services are a unique combination of Spirit-sensitive planning and well-managed unpredictability.

The praise and worship time at the beginning of the service lasts anywhere from 30 minutes to an hour, and no one would object if it took over the whole service. During worship, trained lay ministers—or "prayer ushers" I like to call them—are available to pray individually with anyone who has a need. Many people of all ages take advantage of the prayer time, resulting in some free-flowing movement during praise and worship. The activity doesn't seem to bother the others though, who are focused on worshiping the Lord. When necessary, individuals who are very distraught, or simply need an extended time of personal prayer are led into a prayer room off the sanctuary for privacy.

The messages are spiritually challenging and scriptural, sometimes edgy. The pastor's love for Jesus and passion for the lost are clearly evident in just about every sermon he preaches. He frequently addresses local, national and global issues, and strives to help his people peek through the curtain to see the spiritual significance of such events. He wants them to see the world down to the smallest detail as God sees it, and feel his heart in every circumstance. His sermons are unapologetic about the truth, yet delivered in a spirit of patience and love. Listeners leave with a sense of hope and anticipation about what God is doing in the world and in their own lives.

Following the message there is another ministry time in which people are invited to respond to the message in their seats or at the altar. Every week, people are saved and set free in response to the gospel. The prayer ushers are available to pray and minister for as long as needed, even long after the service has been dismissed. A couple of special places in the church have been designated and comfortably furnished just for this purpose.

In addition to being devoted to personal ministry, the Mary church seems almost fanatical about worship. It's a big part of who they are as a church. It plays a big role not only during the regular worship services, but in other aspects of church life as well. For example, the church board spends time worshiping during their monthly meetings. Four to six times a year, the church holds a 24-hour worship vigil during which they have continual worship in the sanctuary. As often as he can, the pastor brings in worship leaders and guest musicians for concerts and special events. And a variety of worship CD's and tapes can be purchased in the foyer on Sundays, and through the church office during the week.

For most of the regular members, Sunday morning worship is just an extension of their lives during the week. Many have learned to practice worship as a lifestyle, in their cars, at home, even on the job. The music minister believes his primary job is to model worship and teach the people how to worship individually, so that when they come together corporately, he and the other musicians act as facilitators and not entertainers. He tries hard to keep worship focused on Jesus, and resist the tendency to slip into "performance mode." With a lot of incredibly talented musicians on his team, that's not always easy! They spend much time in prayer before each service and keep individual talent shows to a minimum.

Worship in the Mary church is not just about music, however. The pastor challenges his people to find other ways to express worship such as bowing or lying before the Lord, waiting in silence, or reading creeds, written prayers, poems or hymns out loud. He makes song books, hymnals and worship CD's available to the people for use at home; he wants to surround them with good worship tools. He strives to be creative to keep worship fresh and alive, but also likes to draw on their spiritual heritage and embrace some time honored traditions. He's open to anything that brings attention to Jesus and lifts up his name.

No matter what the expression, worship in the Mary church is very "Godward," utilizing primarily what I call prayer songs—songs in which the lyrics are sung *to* God instead of *about* God. The focus is on God, not on the music minister, any one performer or even the worship team as a group. This style of worship is very intimate because it is not just about singing songs, but about communing with God and sensing his resulting nearness. Sometimes people are moved to kneel at their seats or move to the altar. Some raise their hands or clap. Even a long period of silence, which would have an awkward and uncomfortable feel in most churches, would be a welcomed form of worship and not particularly out of character. In short, worship in the Mary church has elements of emotion and passion fitting for an encounter between bride and bridegroom.

...worship in the Mary church has elements of emotion and passion fitting for an encounter between bride and bridegroom.

Because of the active nature of worship and the open feel of personal ministry, the Mary church may seem, especially to visitors, to be less organized or polished than its Martha counterpart. It doesn't have a "production" feel to it, and some may even describe it as unstructured. This is because the Mary service is not a performance for the people, but rather an offering to God by the people.

Another thing that one might notice about the Mary church is that many people have stories to tell about how God has changed either their lives, or the life of a loved one. It has a reputation for being a place where interesting things are always happening. People are saved, healed and set free from illnesses and addictions during the worship and prayer times on Sunday, as well as in the various small groups that meet during the week. It's almost as though the people have an unusual openness or vulnerability because they come expecting something more than a sermon. They come to participate and receive, not just watch.

For example, just a few months ago, a woman who had been diagnosed with cancer was healed following months of prayer by the church body, including a prayer vigil in her behalf. Several doctors confirmed both the initial diagnosis and the fol-low-up reports that there was no longer any evidence of cancer in her body. Since then, she has been praying and ministering to other individuals and families facing cancer or dealing with losses from the disease.

Testimonies like this one of people being helped or healed in significant ways are so powerful that it is not uncommon for others who are struggling with life to seek out the church in the hopes of receiving the same kind of compassion and prayer. And even though not every story ends in physical healing, the Mary church never stops praying. Their faith in God's ability and good-ness isn't affected by outcomes they don't understand. They are not concerned about their reputation; they just trust Jesus.

The Mary church has also commissioned many of its own

members over the years into some kind of full time ministry in response to God's calling on their lives. It seems to be a launching pad for new pastors and missionaries. Many have entered the mission field, gone on to be pastors in other places, or become involved in parachurch ministries within the community because of their involvement with the church.

The Mary church doesn't do a lot of mass mailing in the area to advertise programs and activities. In fact, they don't really market—at least not through traditional means—much at all. Many from the spiritually curious to the desperately needy find their way to the church through friends or special events and as a result, the church shows steady growth.

The congregation is more diverse than some of the other churches in the area because the common denominator is not ethnicity or social status, but rather the bond of grace received and grace given. In the Mary church, a lawyer worships next to a waitress; an ex-con worships next to a young seminary student. Titles and credentials are checked at the door.

Visitors generally find the church to be a warm and welcoming place, but the protocol is not defined by them. The flow of worship and ministry is attached to something bigger than the church itself, like a boat being carried down a river that stops or changes course for no one. The stream of worship gently washes over anyone who steps into the flow and respectfully passes by those who choose to stay at a distance. No one is cajoled or pressured. Visitors are drawn into the church not by persuasion but by the enticing sounds on the deck as the boat passes by.

Like the Martha church, activity in the Mary church is certainly not relegated to Sundays. Various small groups within the church use the building for meetings each week, as do a few local organizations supported by the church. One of these is a ministry to battered women founded by one of the church members several years ago following her own dramatic conversion to Christ. A former victim of domestic violence, she stumbled upon help and hope at a Mary church special event when someone said, "Can I pray for you?" That night, her life was so radically transformed that she is now rescuing other young women in despair.

It is testimonies like these, of lives completely covered by the grace of God, which seem to be the joy of the Mary church. Their "plaques of achievement" are the walking miracles in their midst that tell the story of Jesus' power to heal and redeem. Individual contributions are acknowledged and celebrated, but are quickly and willingly swept into the current of humility that starts with the pastor and flows throughout the congregation. "It's all about Jesus," the pastor explains. "It's not about what people can do."

One of the busiest places during the week is the prayer room. People come and go on the hour, some staying for two or three hours at a time. They pray around the stations in the room that cover such themes as government leaders, current events, local police and firefighters, hospitals, churches, businesses and schools in the area, individual prayer requests submitted by church members, and the pastoral staff and their families. Some pray over the many lists, maps and information that are provided, while others prefer to simply worship.

The Mary church also has a wide variety of other prayer ministries that one can be involved in. For example, each pastor on staff has a team of personal intercessors that pray regularly for him and his family. Teams arrive an hour before every service to walk through the sanctuary inviting God's Presence, while another group prays in the same manner during the services in the prayer room. A special workplace prayer ministry targets local businesses using community prayer request boxes, and another prayer ministry covers every home in the city with prayer over the course of each calendar year. And of course there is a team of crisis intercessors that can be called into action when personal tragedies arise in the congregation or in times of special corporate need.

Many of this church's prayer efforts focus in one way or another on reaching the lost—a mission so important to this church that it is a part of their statement of purpose. Because reaching the lost is such a passion for the pastor and his people, about one third of the church's membership actually joined as newly converted Christians. Many are not only young in their faith, they are experiencing church for the first time as well, and that's the way the pastor likes it. "They may not understand a lot about church etiquette, but they sure are excited about Jesus," he says. Anytime someone makes a new commitment to Christ, it's cause for celebration.

When the prayer ministries really began to take off a couple of years ago, the pastor hired Mary as a full time prayer coordinator to oversee the big picture. Each of the different prayer expressions has its own captain that reports to Mary, and together the captains make up a prayer task force that meets once a month to pray and plan. They try to keep things fresh and interesting by rotating prayer opportunities throughout the year and introducing new ones from time to time. They also recruit and train new prayer ushers each year during the annual "prayer pledge campaign."

Prayer, like worship, is not just an activity in the Mary church; it is woven into the very fabric of all that the church is and does. The leadership strategy and decision making process are no exception. The official governing board of the church seldom votes on issues—instead they allow the process of prayer and seeking to bring them to a place of consensus. In fact, when they meet together, much of their time is spent in corporate prayer and worship.

When the board faces decisions about the vision and direction of the church, there may be some differing opinions at the outset. But they don't park there and jockey for support; they pray. As a group and as individuals, they are committed to laying the circumstance before the Lord and asking for his guidance. Sometimes it takes only a few moments during the course of a meeting, and other times they pray and seek God for weeks before a decision is reached. But in either case, their hearts are drawn into agreement by the promptings of the Holy Spirit. Because the congregation knows their leadership is seeking God fervently in this manner, most decisions are readily embraced by the majority and are often further confirmed in wonderful ways through the church body.

This is not to say that the church is perfect or that it never has to deal with any kind of disagreement. Just like the Martha church, it is made up of people who have ideas and opinions that don't always line up. Individuals get offended or disgruntled in the Mary church just as they do in any other human organization. The road is not always smooth.

For example, not long ago, a very well-respected couple in the church confronted the pastor because of a decision made by the church leadership. It was clearly time to have some work done on the exterior of one of the church buildings and the husband owned a company that could do the job. However, after praying for direction, instead of utilizing the services of the husband's company, the leaders all felt the strong urging of the Holy Spirit to hire a different company run by non-believers. They knew it didn't appear to make logical sense, but they trusted in their discernment.

The pastor did his best to explain this to his church member, a man whom he truly loved and respected, but the man was having a hard time accepting what he felt was rejection, and in his mind, a poor decision. After all, he had given faithfully to support the church, and now he felt they were being disloyal in return.

Although the situation was awkward and difficult, it was eventually resolved and the couple stayed. Though he never wavered about the word the leadership team felt they had received in prayer, the pastor was sensitive to the man's feelings and welcomed his input. The two of them prayed together, and the man ultimately trusted in his pastor's spiritual leadership and ability to hear from God. Most significantly, the incident was not allowed to become a control struggle because the pastor's focus was on hearing from God, not discrediting his friend.

The Mary Pastor

Like his church, the Mary pastor is different. He's not your typical organizational manager, held hostage in his own life by the tyranny of urgent phone calls and endless committee meetings. He is a different kind of leader, more gifted in receiving and casting vision than analyzing the church budget; more excited about new baptisms than a record offering on Sunday morning. His people respect his leadership because they know he is diligent about getting alone with God and seeking his direction.

Because the Mary pastor's first priority is his personal devotion life, he is not nearly as visible as his Martha counterpart. He does keep regular office hours to take care of weekly scheduled appointments, and he lends leadership to several key ministries within the church, but don't expect to see him at every fellowship function mingling like a campaigning politician. And don't look for him much at all on Fridays, Saturdays or Mondays. Friday and Saturday are his preparation days and Monday is his day off to spend with his family, and on these days he frequently draws apart to one of several nearby retreats to pray.

On the days (Tuesday through Thursday) when he is in the

office, he doesn't take appointments until 10:00 because he commits the first several hours of each day to meet with God. While he sometimes worries that church business needs more of his time and attention, he knows that if he gets too far from his prayer closet, he's vulnerable to all sorts of distractions. He might get sucked into the swirling abyss of people and problems and never resurface. With each year that passes, he feels more and more aware of his own weaknesses, and therefore more and more dependent on God's anointing to lead his church. A couple of times a year, he takes an extended time away for personal retreat and spiritual refreshment.

To help him stay before God, he built a team around him of staff and lay leaders who are well trained, equipped and commissioned to handle most ministry situations that many other senior pastors deal with themselves, so that he can spend more time seeking, studying and worshiping. In addition, he finds ways to intentionally show his congregation how to rely on each other and the lay ministers instead of him in their times of need.

While the Mary pastor stays in touch with every facet of the church ministry and accepts responsibility for all the aspects of church administration, he is not a micromanager. He trusts his leaders in their various roles and he enthusiastically blesses and supports their efforts. Because they pray and worship together regularly as a team, he feels confident in their respective visions and knows that they are moving with God's guidance.

The youth minister, for example, holds a Friday night worship service targeting teens, college students and some young married couples. The format of the service is very different from that of Sunday morning, and the pastor has little involvement in any part of the activity. Yet the service is growing and people are being ministered to, and he loves hearing the reports about what God is doing through the creativity and faithfulness of his young associate. He doesn't feel the need to control it or even completely understand it because he knows that the youth minister is seeking and hearing God.

They don't expect him to be at their beck and call or to be their best friend.

The people have been taught that their pastor's job is to be with God, and so although he carries a cell phone, it rarely rings. When crises arise, they are more likely to call one of the prayer leaders that are very visible in the church, or perhaps their small group leader. They don't expect him to be at their beck and call or to be their best friend.

Spending so much time out of the fray in his personal "tent of meeting" influences the Mary pastor in several ways. For example, because he spends time waiting on God, his spiritual senses are sharp and he receives fresh revelation about the Word and the things God is doing today. As a result, the messages he brings to the pulpit Sunday after Sunday are vibrant and revelatory, poured out of his own overflowing cup. His words, whether they soothe like salve or cut like a laser, give hope and conviction to everyone who hears. Lots of people leave saying, "Wow, you really hit the nail on the head today," or "That really spoke to my situation." When Jesus is lifted up and the gospel is preached with authority and insight, the results are manifold on many different levels.

Second, the Mary pastor feels refreshed and renewed, more excited about ministry than ever before. He is optimistic and peaceful, and his passion for Jesus and his calling grows with each passing year. While some of his peers are already talking wistfully about retirement, he feels "refired" and enthusiastic about the future. He is bold in proclaiming the things God shows him and innovative in ministering to his church and the surrounding community. Instead of scouring the pages of the latest best seller or recycling ideas from model "mega" churches around the country—he's sitting at the feet of the Master and saying, "I don't want to move without your mandate. Show me your heart."

Another result of his time with the Lord is that the Mary pastor is less affected by the opinions of people because he is constantly getting God's opinion. When he and his leadership team evaluate the services, his basic questions are always the same, "Did God show up? Did he feel welcome to manifest himself? Were people healed and touched? Did they experience him?" What people think is very secondary. Because he doesn't feel pressured to solve everyone's problem and offer a solution for every need, he's free to minister in the places God truly leads him.

When he is in the public eye, the Mary pastor speaks blessing and life. He prays regularly with a group of pastors in town, and they know him as a humble, generous man. He always speaks highly of other churches in his area and does what he can to encourage trust, unity, accountability and friendship among the various pastors. He has gone out of his way to try and build relationships with several local pastors who seem isolated from the city-wide fellowship. Though not everyone understands or appreciates his efforts, many recognize him as a leader within the church community. Several of the younger pastors in his area see him as a mentor and role model.

The Mary church pastor is respected in part because he has a well-earned reputation for supporting other churches that are in need. His commitment to a strong pastoral network is not just rhetoric. He puts his money where his mouth is. He has called on his church to paint signs for churches that didn't have one, scholarship pastors of small churches to renewal conferences or retreats, and even supplement pastors' salaries when he saw the need. Not long ago, when an older downtown church of a different denomination was damaged by vandalism, he contributed both manpower and significant cash to help them repair the damage and restore their building. He reasons that promoting other churches in the community and helping them succeed is a good strategy because it honors God.

The Mary pastor is a creative leader who strives to follow the leading of the Holy Spirit, even when it seems contrary to public opinion or tradition. Though cautious and discerning when it comes to protecting his flock, he is not afraid to take risks or try different approaches. He knows God is doing new things all the time and he doesn't want his church to miss out. He believes in moving forward, and refuses to live in the past.

The Presence Based Church

The Mary church can be big or little, denominational or independent, liturgical or contemporary. I have seen "Mary" in churches of all sizes and flavors. Regardless of the façade, though, Mary churches are, at their core, what I call Presence based churches.

To be Presence based is basically to be completely dependent on God's Presence for everything. Or to turn it around, to be Presence based means that without God's Presence, the church would cease to exist. It is to be God's chosen people, his favorites, whom he longs to be with and who long to be with him.

The Presence based church is a movement. It's not my movement, but something that the Holy Spirit is stirring up in hearts of believers today. As a model, it is difficult to describe because the essence of it doesn't lie so much in the visible realm of church life, but somewhere beneath the songs, suppers and sermons, deep in the hearts and spirits of the individual worshipers. It is what this book is all about, but to fully explain it, I first have to take you on a side journey—an expedition—that will lay the groundwork for much of what I want to say from here on out. But please remember this reference point because I will come back here.

Our journey is a tour through the desert with a shepherd named Moses and a congregation whose destiny it was to be the pioneers in our spiritual history.

Discussion Questions

1. Have you ever experienced a Mary church? Where do you see the heart of Mary in your own church?

2. How diverse is your congregation? Why is diversity a characteristic of the Mary church?

3. If you were to poll your congregation, would they prefer your pastor to spend an hour in his prayer closet, or show up at the weekly fellowship dinners?

4. Does anything about the Mary church description make you uncomfortable? Explain.

5. Which word would better characterize the decision making process in your church: agreement or disagreement? How often do you feel that God has his way in your church:

    Almost always - "I know our leaders are hearing God!"

    Sometimes - "We want to please both God and people."

    Almost never - "I'm afraid the sheep are running the shed."

6. What part of the Sunday morning service at your church causes you to worship? Do you ever worship when you're not at church?

7. What is "Godward" worship?

THE PRESENCE

When God was leading the Israelites out of captivity and through their desert tour, he told their leader Moses, "My Presence will go with you, and I will give you rest" (Exodus 33:14). Moses responded:

> If your Presence does not go with us, do not send us up from here. How will anyone know that you are pleased with me and with your people unless you go with us? What else will distinguish me and your people from all the other people on the face of the earth? (Exodus 33:15-16)

Moses considered the Presence of God to be the most important ingredient he needed to be successful at what God was asking him to do. He also knew that the Presence was what would set them apart as God's chosen, beloved nation. He was not concerned about money, supplies or desert wandering experience. He did not seem to care much about the size of his army or the less than ideal accommodations. He never asked God for more knowledge or power or authority over the sometimes stubborn and rebellious people he was leading. All he really wanted was to know that God's Presence was with him.

When God first called Moses to lead the people out of Egypt, Moses wasn't sure he had the credentials to pull it off. So he asked God, "Suppose I go to the Israelites and say to them, 'The God of your fathers has sent me to you,' and they ask me, 'What is his name?' Then what shall I tell them?" And God answered, "I AM WHO I AM. This is what you are to say to the Israelites: I AM has sent me to you" (Exodus 3:13-14).

"I AM" is a powerful expression of the Presence. The verb "am" communicates being, and God is the essence and ground of all being in heaven and on the earth. I AM is to be, and to be is to have presence.

So what exactly is the Presence of God? Can it even be defined? Talking about presence is difficult because it is not a tangible thing we can see and put our hands on. By nature, it is a somewhat mysterious concept. To try and describe God's Presence is like taking a picture of the Grand Canyon with a Polaroid at night. What you get is a vague representation at best of the original wonder. God's Presence defies the limits of our vocabulary and dwarfs our most unbridled imaginations. Known and yet unknown, it will remain a profoundly wonderful mystery until we see him full of glory in heaven.

It is said that before George Frideric Handel, the German composer, wrote *Messiah*, he prayed and sought God's inspiration and blessing. He penned the entire masterpiece in only 24 days. The notes flowed from his mind almost faster than he could get them on paper. When he finished, he emerged from his study with tears streaming down his face and said to his servant, "I did tink I did see all heffen before me, und da great Gott himself!"[1]

The Presence of God is quintessential energy unlike anything in this world. It is spiritual in nature, but more real than what we believe to be real. As a starting point for understanding, let us think for a minute about the word "presence." Consider these definitions of presence from the dictionary:

1. The state or fact of being present; current existence or occurrence.

2. Immediate proximity in time or space.

3. The area immediately surrounding a great personage, especially a sovereign.

4. A person who is present.

5a. A person's bearing, especially when it commands respectful attention: *She has such presence that she lights up the room....* **b.** The quality of self-assurance and effectiveness that permits a performer to achieve a rapport with the audience: *stage presence.*

6. A supernatural influence felt to be nearby.

7. The diplomatic, political, or military influence of a nation in a foreign country, especially as evidenced by the posting of its diplomats or its troops there: *The American presence in Iraq....*[2]

Each of these definitions has interesting application when talking about the Presence of God. His Presence is real and current, and its proximity in time and space can be felt or detected. It emanates directly from God himself, commanding respectful attention from all that it envelopes. Powerful yet eternally good, severely sovereign yet inviting, God's Presence is the full measure of his being that radiates from himself, enabling him to interact with us personally and influence our fragile human existence. It is the essence and reality of his personhood.

The Presence is to God himself as the rays are to the sun, a precise representation of the source at a much lower intensity level. It is an enormous planet among thousands of swirling galaxies—the pinnacle of an iceberg that reaches miles and miles below the water's surface. It is a glimmer of who God is, lovingly revealed so that we may give ourselves in worship to him.

Frank Damazio, in his book *The Gate Church*, says this about the Presence:

> The Hebrew word "presence," *paniym*, is used seventy-six times in the Old Testament. It is derived from the root word *panah*, meaning "to turn" or "to turn the face toward." This word denotes the blessing and favor of God turned toward those who worship Him. The presence of God is a presence that fills up, pervades, permeates and overspreads all who come under it.[3]

To see a person's face is to gaze into the window of their presence. When we seek God's Presence, we are seeking his face or his countenance. We are seeking to know him as we might know our spouse or our child. Being "face to face" or touching a person's face is a very intimate, vulnerable experience.

Concealed in Clouds

Scripture, especially the Old Testament, teaches us several things about The Presence of God. One pattern we see is that God often shrouds the effulgence of his Presence in a cloud. He told Moses, "I am going to come to you in a dense cloud, so that the people will hear me speaking with you and will always put their trust in you" (Exodus 19:3). Exodus 34:5-6 describes how "the LORD came down in the cloud and stood there with him and proclaimed his name, the LORD. And he passed in front of Moses...." The cloud of God's Presence descended on the tabernacle in the wilderness (Leviticus 16:2; Numbers 9:15), and in the temple (1 Kings 8:10-12; 2 Chronicles 5:13-14).

"I AM WHO I AM. This is what you are to say to the Israelites: I AM has sent me to you."

I sometimes think of God's Presence concealed in a cloud when I look out the window of an airplane. He chose a majestic wardrobe! From dark, foreboding thunderheads to playful white shapes and wisps of cotton, clouds seem the perfect creation to express every mood and whim of the creator himself. They can blanket the sky like a cover of down or bounce along a vivid blue backdrop. They can paint the most resplendent works of art in a sunrise or a sunset. Spectacular as they are, it is no wonder that God chose clouds as his earthly attire.

Revealed in Fire

Just as God used clouds to *conceal* the full effect of his Presence, the Bible tells us that he used fire to *reveal* his Presence:

> By day the LORD went ahead of them in a pillar of cloud to guide them on their way and by night in a pillar of fire to give them light, so that they could travel by day or night. Neither the pillar of cloud by day nor the pillar of fire by night left its place in front of the people (Exodus 13:21-22).

The fire of his Presence became known as the "consuming fire" (Deuteronomy 4:24)—a holy fire, representing the total power and purity of God's being. No sin could remain in its midst. This consuming fire came as a judgment on the people when they doubted God's appointed leader in Moses (Numbers 16:35), and when they complained about their hardships (Numbers 11:1-3). It came down from heaven and consumed their offerings when they made sacrifices to the Lord (Leviticus 9:24). It distinguished them from all others.

Upon completion of the permanent temple that would house the Ark of the Covenant, the designated resting place of

God's Presence, Solomon prayed a prayer of dedication and God descended in fire, filling the temple to such an extent that no one could go near:

> When Solomon finished praying, fire came down from heaven and consumed the burnt offering and the sacrifices, and the glory of the LORD filled the temple. The priests could not enter the temple of the LORD because the glory of the LORD filled it. When all the Israelites saw the fire coming down and the glory of the LORD above the temple, they knelt on the pavement with their faces to the ground, and they worshiped and gave thanks to the LORD, saying, "He is good; his love endures forever." (2 Chronicles 7:1-3).

Imagine what it would be like today if the glory of the Lord were to fill a church to such an extent that no one could even go near! It would make the national news. If people flock to see an image of the Virgin Mary in a glass window or a tree, how many would rush to a church building where God himself was so real that his Presence was almost tangible?

Terrible and Terrifying

Notice what the Israelites did when they encountered the Presence—they "knelt on the pavement with their faces to the ground." Scripture consistently confirms that in addition to being associated with clouds and fire, God's Presence always elicited a dramatic fear response in men. It was literally terrifying.

Exodus 19:16-19 describes a surreal scene that took place on the edge of the Israelite camp:

> On the morning of the third day there was thunder and lightning, with a thick cloud over the mountain, and a very loud trumpet blast. Everyone in the camp trembled. Then Moses led the people out of the camp to meet with God, and they stood at the foot of the mountain. Mount Sinai was covered with smoke, because the LORD descended on it in fire. The smoke billowed up from it like smoke from a furnace, the whole mountain trembled violently, and the sound of the trumpet grew louder and louder. Then Moses spoke and the voice of God answered him.

This was hardly a church service you could have slept through! Before the days of lasers, computer animation and special effects, it was a display even Hollywood would have been proud of. For the Israelites, to whom a flashlight would have seemed mysterious, a glowing, smoking, musical mountain must have been horrifying. It is easy to understand why we read in Exodus 20:18-19:

> When the people saw the thunder and lightning and heard the trumpet and saw the mountain in smoke, they trembled with fear. They stayed at a distance and said to Moses, "Speak to us yourself and we will listen. But do not have God speak to us or we will die.

Even during times of celebration, the Presence evoked a characteristic response of absolute humility and fearful submission (Leviticus 9:24). Philip Yancey is right when he says that reading in Exodus and Leviticus the precise instructions for constructing the temple and its furnishings, one gets the impression that the Presence must be approached like highly radioactive material.[4] The meticulous detail in which these structures are described indicates the seriousness of the business! God did not take the construction of his official resting place lightly, nor did he leave any decision up to the whimsy of the builders. Consider, for example, this description of part of the temple courtyard:

> The curtain for the entrance to the courtyard was of blue, purple and scarlet yarn and finely twisted linen—the work of an embroiderer. It was twenty cubits long and, like the curtains of the courtyard, five cubits high, with four posts and four bronze bases. Their hooks and bands were silver, and their tops were overlaid with silver. All the tent pegs of the tabernacle and of the surrounding courtyard were bronze (Exodus 38:18-20).

The instructions for priests were equally painstaking, including what they were to wear, how they were to be consecrated for ministry, and some of their responsibilities. God instructed Moses that his brother Aaron and his sons were to be set apart as priests. The skilled artisans were to make the following sacred garments using gold, blue, purple and scarlet yarn and fine linen: a breastpiece, an ephod (sleeveless vestment), a robe, a woven tunic, a turban and a sash. These are just a few of the specifications for the breastpiece:

It is to be square—a span long and a span wide—
and folded double. Then mount four rows of precious stones on it. In the first row there shall be a
ruby, a topaz and a beryl; in the second row a tur-
quoise, a sapphire and an emerald; in the third row a
jacinth, an agate and an amethyst; in the fourth row
a chrysolite, an onyx and a jasper. Mount them in
gold filigree settings. There are to be twelve stones,
one for each of the names of the sons of Israel,
each engraved like a seal with the name of one of
the twelve tribes (Exodus 28:15-43).

God's instructions were specific, and he expected them to
be strictly followed. Any deviation was unacceptable in his Presence. As a result, the job of priest carried with it both a high
degree of honor and a high degree of risk, and was certainly not
a job for anyone with authority issues. For example, two of Aaron's
sons were struck dead in the temple by the Lord because they
"offered unauthorized fire" in the burning of incense contrary
to his command (Leviticus 10:1-2). After fire from the Presence
of God consumed the boys, the Bible says, "Aaron remained silent" (Leviticus 10:3). I have often wondered what he was thinking as he looked upon his two sons. And I have wondered what
might be classified as "unauthorized fire" in churches today.

Because one slip up basically meant barbecue, some histo-
rians believe that it became common practice to tie a rope around
the priest's ankle before he entered into the Presence and place a
bell on his garment. The people would stay outside the temple

watching and listening. As long as they could hear the jingle of the bell, they knew the priest was okay. But if the priest died, they had to have a way to retrieve the body. Since they didn't dare enter into the temple themselves, they would drag his body out by the rope. It would have been almost impossible for a priest to get good life insurance.

Many Christians today steer clear of the Old Testament because of passages like these. They do not understand this terrifying aspect of God's nature and can not reconcile it with the idyllic, loving Jesus they know as savior. But as Paul reminded the Romans, we must "behold the goodness *and* severity of God…" (Romans 11:22 NASB, italics mine). When he says, "behold" he is saying, "take note, don't forget, acknowledge." We will have a distorted view of God and his plan for salvation if we do not deal with all parts of his character. While we are thankfully living under grace and not the law today, God's nature has not changed.

> *We will have a distorted view of God and his plan for salvation if we do not deal with all parts of his character.*

The Voice of God

Finally, if the Presence was nebulous in clouds and awesome in fire, it was unmistakably precise in voice. Old Testament

Scripture tells us that God often revealed his Presence by speaking directly to Moses in his own words:

> The LORD would speak to Moses face to face, as a man speaks with his friend (Exodus 33:11).

> When Moses entered the Tent of Meeting to speak with the LORD, he heard the voice speaking to him from between the two cherubim above the atonement cover on the ark of the Testimony. And he spoke with him (Numbers 7:89).

Much of the content of the first five books of the Bible starts with the phrase, "The LORD said to Moses…." In the tabernacle, the Presence became the Israelites' teacher, instructing, training and disciplining this unleavened people. In the Ten Commandments, he gave them rules for safe living and peaceful co-existence. It was Life 101. He taught them about personal relationships and how to deal with injuries. He spoke about protection of property and etiquette. He settled disputes. He gave details about social responsibility and advice for staying healthy. He told them about safe sex and how to get water. He gave instructions on worship and the proper presentation of offerings. He designed the priests' clothes. He even let Moses know when he was angry, like when he told him, "Get away from this assembly so I can put an end to them at once!" (Numbers 16:45)

God spoke with power and purpose. He spoke and the desert shook. He had a lot to say. It's amazing that Moses remembered and recorded everything he heard without a laptop or PDA!

When God spoke, he expected the people to listen and obey. To hear and heed was to prosper. To hear and disobey was to suffer (Deuteronomy 28). He made the choice clear, "...I have set before you life and death, blessings and curses. Now choose life, so that you and your children may live and that you may love the LORD your God, listen to his voice, and hold fast to him" (Deuteronomy 30:19-20).

Israel – A Presence Based People

As a result of their unique relationship with God, the Israelites became the original Presence based people. Under the leadership of Moses, and at God's bidding, they made the Presence the axis of their lives.

The Ark of the Covenant was always located in the tabernacle at the very center of the camp. The 12 tribes were divided into four groups and stationed symmetrically around the Presence: three to the north, three to the south, three to the east and three to the west. By day they saw the cloud that hung over the tent, and by night they would lie in the entrance to their own tents and watch the fire. As long as the Presence stayed, they stayed. But when the Presence moved, they followed. They were Presence led and Presence drawn.

Since ministering to the Presence was Israel's top priority, one entire tribe was assigned the privilege of caring for and guarding the Ark. The Levites, as they were called, worked closely with the priests around the clock ministering to the Lord. Twenty-two thousand men strong, the Levites attended to the Presence day and night, worshiping and waiting on the Lord (Numbers 3:39). They guarded its precious place in their lives.

The book of Numbers outlines the Levites' roles as ministers to the tabernacle. The Levites were of the tribe Levi, chosen by God to represent the other eleven tribes before the Lord (Numbers 3:41, 45). Assigned the responsibility of erecting, dismantling and carrying the tabernacle, including the Ark of the Covenant, the Levites received no land inheritance as the other tribes did. Instead, the Lord said that he himself would be their inheritance (Deuteronomy 10:9). Deuteronomy 10:8 underscores the Levites' importance, "At that time the LORD set apart the tribe of Levi to carry the ark of the covenant of the LORD, to stand before the LORD to minister and to pronounce blessings in his name…." The Revised Standard Version of the Bible refers to them as Levitical priests.

By the time King Solomon built the permanent temple, music had become a significant part of the Levitical job description. As the Ark was placed in the inner sanctuary, we read:

> All the Levites who were musicians—Asaph, Heman, Jeduthun and their sons and relatives—stood on the east side of the altar, dressed in fine linen and playing cymbals, harps and lyres. They were accompanied by 120 priests sounding trumpets. The trumpeters and singers joined in unison, as with one voice, to give praise and thanks to the LORD. Accompanied by trumpets, cymbals and other instruments, they raised their voices in praise to the LORD and sang:

"He is good; his love endures forever" (2 Chronicles 5:12-13).

It was David, Solomon's father, who incorporated music into the Levites' ministry in the Presence. David knew full well the wonder and lure of the Presence, and he expressed it in many of the Psalms he wrote:

> How lovely is your dwelling place, O LORD Almighty! My soul yearns, even faints, for the courts of the LORD; my heart and my flesh cry out for the living God. Better is one day in your courts than a thousand elsewhere... (Psalm 84:1-2, 10).

Worship and praise became part of the daily order before the Presence. They would play and sing to the Lord as they waited on him day and night. Interestingly, the Hebrew word for wait means to "bind together, be tethered to, or look longingly with patience." That is what the Levites and priests did—bound themselves to God and longingly looked for his revelation.

Notice that the priests' job was not to minister to the people, but to the Presence. And they did so 24-7, not just from 11:00 to 12:00 on Sunday mornings. How different that seems when we compare it to a typical day in the life of a pastor or priest today.

Israel – A Divine Habitation

If you stopped reading here, you might wonder, "Why would anyone have *wanted* the job of priest? God seemed awfully hard to get along with—almost ruthless." Reminds me of the scene in the Wizard of Oz when Dorothy and her friends approach the wizard, trembling, wide-eyed, huddled together, fearing that each step could be their last.

However, God's relationship with the people of Israel was a very special one. Inasmuch as God was absolutely holy, just and righteous, he was also devoted, passionate and loyal toward them. If he seemed harsh in discipline, it was because his paternal love for these people ran deep, and like every good father, he knew what was best. He was and is both wholly good and wholly severe. The Israelites were sloppy, irresponsible and disobedient at times, but they were his children. They knew exactly what was expected and when they didn't fall in line, the consequences were sure and swift.

Ever since God created Adam and Eve, his desire has been to spend time with mankind.

Ever since God created Adam and Eve, his desire has been to spend time with mankind. He created us for his pleasure, in his image. Now he chose the Israelites from among all the peoples on the earth, and he set them apart to be *his* people. He told them, "Now if you obey me fully and keep my covenant, then out of all nations you will be my treasured possession. Although the whole earth is mine, you will be for me a kingdom of priests and a holy nation" (Exodus 19:5-6; see also Exodus 7:6).

Moses explained to the people why the Lord had chosen them to be his nation:

The LORD did not set his affection on you and choose you because you were more numerous than other peoples, for you were the fewest of all peoples. But it was because the LORD *loved* you and kept the oath he swore to your forefathers... (Exodus 7:7-8, italics mine; see also 4:20).

What a humbling thought—to be God's "treasured possession" and object of his affection, for no other reason except that he wanted it that way.

One of the scenes that I think best illustrates God's heart about the Israelites is in Exodus 24:9-11 when Moses, Aaron, Aaron's two sons (yes, the same two that would later die in the temple) and seventy elders went up on the mountain to be with God. The Bible says, "Under his feet was something like a pavement made of sapphire, clear as the sky itself. But God did not raise his hand against these leaders of the Israelites; they saw God, and they ate and drank." Wow! They actually *saw* God and had lunch together! What an awesome thought.

Moses had several intimate encounters with God. Sometimes the effects of the Presence were actually visible, as when Moses came down from the mountain in Exodus 34 after receiving the Ten Commandments, unaware that his face was "radiant because he had spoken with the LORD" (v. 29). When Aaron and the other leaders saw Moses' face, they were afraid to go near him and they ran away. Poor Moses didn't understand what was wrong, but as soon as someone whispered in his ear that he was glowing, he put a veil over his face so the people would not be afraid. Then he told them all that the Lord had said.

I believe episodes like these kept the Israelites coming back for more. The Presence of God is so delicious that one taste only creates a hunger for more and more. The effects of being in *the* Presence, even for a moment, are life-altering. His Presence penetrates and imprints everything it touches, never to be the same. It is the greatest experience one can have, and God's Presence in Israel's life changed them as a people forever.

Israel – A Divine Stronghold

The Presence was the Israelites' security and delight. They did not possess it; rather it possessed them, giving them the special designation of being God's chosen people. Because of its continual habitation and presence in their lives, the Israelites as a nation became what I would call a divine stronghold. Nurtured by Presence based thought systems and habits, divine strongholds grow in the soil of humility and establish God's kingdom in a given area on earth.

In Israel's case, the divine stronghold came about as a result of prolonged exposure to the manifest Presence of God both directly and through Moses' leadership. As they tasted and experienced the Presence, they began to reflect its influence in their lives. God had his way in their lives, and created a reputation for himself through them. His Presence was so pervasive among them that it became their identity—an identity that was largely represented by God's mysterious earthly throne—the Ark of the Covenant.

Discussion Questions

1. Brainstorm. Compile a list of words that might describe the Presence of God. Read the list out loud.

2. What was the main job of the priests in the tabernacle? What was the main job of the Levites?

3. Have you ever experienced the Presence of God? How did you know?

4. Why did God choose the Israelites? What does this say about his nature?

5. Why should we still study the Old Testament if we are no longer living under the Law?

6. Was/is God cruel?

THE ARK OF THE COVENANT

I f you're an Indiana Jones fan then you understand that the Ark of the Covenant is one of the single most important objects that was ever created out of earthly materials, rivaled only perhaps by the cross. Both were made of wood, and both helped God reveal himself to man. It can not be just coincidence that when Jesus came to earth, he lived and worked as a carpenter.

The Steven Spielberg movie *Raiders of the Lost Ark* was based on a renegade, and not particularly spiritual, archeologist's hunt for the ancient Hebrew treasure. The adventure begins when Indiana Jones is commissioned by the United States government to retrieve the treasure even as a German Nazi team is on the brink of unearthing it themselves. Though the plot is almost completely fictitious, the producers did portray a few things with some degree of accuracy with regard to the Ark: the model replica of the Ark, the way it was moved, and the mysteriously dangerous power it contained.

Derived from the Hebrew word "arown" meaning "chest" or "coffin," the Ark was made at the direction of God through Moses. It was a box of acacia wood 15 feet square that God chose to be his earthly throne—the designated place for his Presence to dwell. Interestingly, the acacia wood used to make the chest was not only the most plentiful in that region; it was very durable and covered with thorns. These thorns may have reinforced the unapproachable majesty and power of Jehovah.[1]

On the top of the Ark, made of pure gold, were two cherubim, or angels, kneeling and facing each other, and whose outspread wings covered their faces. Their position suggested that they were guarding the Presence since it was in between the cherubim that the Lord would come to rest. This lid portion of the Ark was called the Mercy Seat. On the sides of the Ark were four gold rings inserted with long poles with which to carry the Ark, since no one was to touch it.

The Ark sat in the Most Holy Place in the center of the tabernacle surrounded by a curtain or veil, and accessible only to Moses and the priests. It was the focal point of life for the Israelites. God told Moses, "There, above the cover between the two cherubim that are over the ark of the Testimony, I will meet with you and give you all my commands for the Israelites" (Exodus 25:22). In the movie, one of Indiana Jones' closest friends wisely assures the highly experienced archeologist, "The Ark of the Covenant is like nothing you've ever gone after before."

Once a year, a priest would enter the Holy of Holies to offer a blood sacrifice on the Mercy Seat as atonement for the Israelites' sin. Once the sacrifice was made, they waited and prayed that God would descend and accept the offering, showing mercy to the people by restoring their oneness with God. Thus, the Mercy Seat was also known as the Seat of Atonement ("at-one-ment"), or Atonement Covering.

The priests who served in the tabernacle were privileged because they could get close to the Ark where God rested. They wore high collars to remind themselves that they were not allowed to rent their clothes in lamentation—a common practice for the grieving. Such a display would not have been fitting for one who had access to the Presence. They were special and chosen by God to fulfill the unique role of mediator.

The Ark contained three physical objects: the Ten Commandments God had given to Moses on the mountain, Aaron's budded rod symbolizing God's authority, and manna which represented God's provision for the people.

We know from the biblical record that the Ark was moved several times throughout Israel's history. Once it was even captured and held for several months by the Philistines. However, the Philistines quickly returned the Ark to Israel when they determined that God's hand was against them in the form of tumors and death because of his dwelling place in their midst.

Several years later when David became king of Israel, he decided the Ark needed to be brought back to the city of Jerusalem and a place of prominence in the nation to acknowledge the Lord's rule over himself and the people. So he gathered 30,000 men to go and bring it up from Judah.

Unfortunately, David had failed to consult the owner's manual, and he was transporting the Ark on a new cart made by the Philistines instead of by the poles as the Lord had commanded. Along the path, when one of the oxen stumbled, a man named Uzzah reached out his hand to steady the chest and immediately died. David became frightened and halted the journey until he could figure out what he was doing wrong. Then he safely brought the Ark the rest of the way into Jerusalem with a great procession of sacrifices, shouts, trumpets and dancing. The Ark was placed in a tent, and would later be moved to the permanent temple built by David's son, King Solomon (2 Samuel 6).

The Ark disappeared in 587 B.C. when the Babylonians invaded Jerusalem. Some say it was destroyed, while others believe it still exists somewhere and will eventually be found.

Purposes of the Ark

The Ark of the Covenant was obviously important because it was the resting place of the Most High God. But it also served several key purposes for the Israelites as God's chosen people.

1. From the Ark, God displayed his power and authority.

God's Presence on the Ark answered any questions about who was in control in the Israelites' camp. The seemingly harsh deaths of Aaron's two sons and Uzzah, because of their mishandling of the Ark, let the people know that as a nation, they existed for God, not vice versa. Time and again he clearly demonstrated his complete and sovereign authority and the power to back it up.

God also gave authority to Moses and Aaron as his appointed leaders of the people, reinforcing it again and again when the Israelites grumbled. They needed no other credentials or titles because they had his official stamp of approval. Moses was a very humble man—"more humble than anyone else on the face of the earth" (Numbers 12:3). (Since Moses is the one who wrote that, I have to wonder if he was really all that humble!) Yet God validated him in front of the people so that they would know his authority was God given: "The LORD said to Moses, 'I am going to come to you in a dense cloud, so that the people will hear me speaking with you and will always put their trust in you'" (Exodus 19:9). Later, God authorized Aaron in front of the whole assembly by causing Aaron's staff to bud, blossom and produce almonds overnight as a miraculous sign of his authority. God instructed Moses to put Aaron's budded staff in the Ark, "to be kept as a sign to the rebellious…so that they will not die" (Numbers 17:1-11).

God's Presence on the Ark answered any questions about who was in control in the Israelites' camp.

God did not take lightly those who questioned his authority or the authority of those he had commissioned. Those who did met with swift and unpleasant consequences. Some were consumed with fire, while others were simply swallowed up by the earth (Numbers 11:1-3; 16:1-35). Ironically, many more would have met with the same fate had Moses not often interceded on their behalf before God. More than once, God was ready to wipe out the whole bunch due to their grumbling against himself and Moses, but Moses pled with God to spare their lives, even as they were talking about stoning him (Numbers 11:2; 14; 15:46-50). Ultimately, the Israelites' rebellion cost them the land which they had been promised (Numbers 14:21-23).

God didn't limit his authority to the Israelites, however. During the time the Ark was held by the Philistines, they placed it in a temple next to their god, which they called Dagon. When they awoke the following morning, the statue of Dagon was on its face in front of the Ark. They put Dagon back in his place. But when they awoke the next day and found the statue not only on its face but completely dismembered, they decided it was time to send the Ark back where it had come from (1 Samuel 5:1-8).

The Ark represented God's total power and authority over all creation. From it, he revealed himself uncensored to the Israelites in order to establish his kingdom among them.

2. From the Ark, God communicated his will to them.

We have already seen how God used the cloud and fire over the tabernacle to guide the Israelites through the desert. When the cloud settled over the tent, the Israelites camped. They did not move until the cloud lifted. Once it did, they followed it without question until it again came to rest above the tabernacle, and then they would pitch their tents again. In this manner, the Israelites were guided by the Presence for forty years. At times, they stayed in the same place for weeks and even months because the cloud would not move from the tent. How much faith and discipline that must have taken for a people looking for their promised land.

God guided the Israelites with fire and clouds, but he governed through his servant Moses with his own voice. It was by communicating so directly with Moses that God reigned in the lives of his people from his throne in the tabernacle:

> When a prophet of the LORD is among you, I reveal myself to him in visions, I speak to him in dreams. But this is not true of my servant Moses; he is faithful in all my house. With him I speak face to face, clearly and not in riddles; he sees the form of the LORD (Numbers 12:6-8).

In *Raiders of the Lost Ark*, one of Indiana Jones' cohorts describes the Ark as a "transmitter—a radio for talking to God."

Never again would anyone have the kind of relationship Moses had with the Lord. God used this time of very direct communication to lay out his rules for living. He gave Moses the Ten Commandments as a code of conduct for the Israelites, and instructed him on many other issues of family and community life.

When conflicts or decisions arose, the priests turned to the Presence for advice and help in discerning the will of God for the people. God told Moses:

Whenever Aaron enters the Holy Place, he will bear
the names of the sons of Israel over his heart on the
breastpiece of decision as a continuing memorial
before the LORD. Also put the Urim and the
Thummim in the breastpiece, so they may be over
Aaron's heart whenever he enters the presence of
the LORD. Thus Aaron will always bear the means of
making decisions for the Israelites over his heart before the LORD (Exodus 28:29-30).

From the Mercy Seat, the Presence of God guided and
governed his chosen people for their own health and prosperity.

**3. From the Ark, his Presence gave them victory over their
enemies.**

Though God had promised the Israelites a land of their
own and given them a great destiny to fulfill, they still had to face
hostile territories and some "giant" obstacles. Some of the people
that stood between them and their new home were not privy to
God's plan, and couldn't have cared less about the desert wan-
derers and their dreams. Many of the armies the Israelites faced
were large in number and stature, and were far better equipped
for battle than the former slaves. But the Presence of God in
their camp would give them victory over even the fiercest enemy.

God told them not to be afraid because he would be with
them (Deuteronomy 1:21). Moses reassured the people:

From heaven he made you hear his voice to discipline you. On earth he showed you his great fire,
and you heard his words from out of the fire. Be-

cause he loved your forefathers and chose their descendants after them, he brought you out of Egypt
by his Presence and his great strength, to drive out
before you nations greater and stronger than you and
to bring you into their land to give it to you for your
inheritance, as it is today (Deuteronomy 4:36-38).

Even as the Israelites were just making their exodus out of
Egypt, the Presence of God in a cloud defeated Pharaoh's army
at the Red Sea, allowing his people to make their escape. Once
the Ark was built, it became the rally point in battle and was
often carried several hundred yards ahead of the people as they
traveled. It made a way for them when there seemed to be no way.

For example, when Joshua was leading the people across
the Jordan, he instructed all the Israelites to fall in line behind the
Levites carrying the Ark. They did as they were told. But the
river was at flood stage and would be too deep and swift to cross.

So when the people broke camp to cross the Jordan,
the priests carrying the ark of the covenant went
ahead of them. Yet as soon as the priests who carried the ark reached the Jordan and their feet touched
the water's edge, the water from upstream stopped
flowing. It piled up in a heap a great distance away....
The priests who carried the ark of the covenant of
the LORD stood firm on dry ground in the middle of
the Jordan, while all Israel passed by until the whole
nation had completed the crossing on dry ground
(Joshua 3:14-17).

When they faced a formidable challenge at the city of Jericho, again the Ark was their key to victory. They marched around the city with the Ark seven times and shouted exactly as the Lord had instructed Joshua to do, and the walls of the city came tumbling down (Joshua 6:6-20).

Of course, it was their faith in God and his Presence with them that brought the Israelites victory, not the box itself. The Israelites learned this lesson the hard way in battle with the Philistines when they were defeated and the Ark was captured. Although God had not forsaken them, he was angry that they had put more trust in the wooden box than in him. They were trying to use the Ark to manipulate God, and as a result he did not grant them the victory that day. They had lost sight of the meaning of the Ark and it had become the object of their worship.

It would have been very easy for the Israelites to see the Ark as some sort of a good luck charm. But of course the Presence was their victory, with or without the Ark, when they were humbled before the Lord. The Ark was only a symbol. The power of his Presence in their behalf is evident in 2 Chronicles 20 when several tribes attacked King Jehoshaphat and his army. Greatly outnumbered, the King cried out to God and God answered:

> Do not be afraid or discouraged because of this vast
> army. For the battle is not yours, but God's. You will
> not have to fight this battle. Take up your positions;
> stand firm and see the deliverance the LORD will give
> you, O Judah and Jerusalem (2 Chronicles 20:15, 17).

Wisely, Jehoshaphat bowed before the Lord and all the

people fell down in worship. He appointed many men to sing to the Lord and praise him for the splendor of his holiness as they went into the battle. At the sound of their worship, God set ambushes against the enemy and they destroyed themselves. The Presence of the Lord gave his people victory even though the Ark was not with them.

4. From the Ark, God's Presence demonstrated his favor and delight for them.

Slavery was the only life the Israelites had ever known. They owned nothing when they set out from Egypt, and they had no idea of just how long and hard their journey would turn out to be. What they did have was God's favor and love.

God expressed his favor toward Israel in many ways. He claimed them as his own chosen people and gave them his name. He entered into a covenant with them, making all that he was and all that he had available to them. He designated them "a kingdom of priests and a holy nation" (Exodus 19:6).

The Lord spoke to them intimately and often. He performed miracles in their behalf, gave them protection from their enemies and provided them water, manna and quail to sustain them. Most significantly, he made his earthly dwelling place among them and revealed himself to them on the Ark of the Testimony. What an amazing gesture of love!

God's favor included his provision. The pot of manna contained in the Ark was a reminder to the Israelites of God's faithfulness to supply even their daily, physical needs. I find it fascinating that during the 40 years that the Israelites wandered in the desert, neither their clothes nor their sandals ever wore out! (Deuteronomy 29:5) I wear out a pair of running shoes in about 6 months and I'm not trekking around in hot sand.

The phrase "face to face" is used five times in the Old Testament to describe the favor between God and his people. I believe when God looked upon his people and his servant Moses, he smiled. The radiance of his smile was an expression of his favor, which he articulated to Moses, proclaiming of himself, "The LORD, the LORD, the compassionate and gracious God, slow to anger, abounding in love and faithfulness, maintaining love to thousands, and forgiving wickedness, rebellion and sin" (Exodus 34:6-7). Then he added:

> *...when God looked upon his people and his servant Moses, he smiled.*

I am making a covenant with you. Before all your people I will do wonders never before done in any nation in all the world. The people you live among will see how awesome is the work that I, the LORD, will do for you (Exodus 34:10).

In the Presence, Moses would pray, "...teach me your ways so I may know you and continue to find favor with you" (Exodus 33:13). Moses, as well as anyone, grasped the incomparable mercy and graciousness of God, that he would bestow the honor of his favor upon any man or nation.

Because his favor was upon the Israelites, God delighted in them and yearned for their love and worship in return. He wanted the relationship to be reciprocal. Inasmuch as he cherished and lavished good things on the people, he wanted them to lavish their praise and affection on him as well. He wanted the Ark of the Covenant to be their rally point for jubilation

As we read many of the Old Testament accounts, it is easy to assume that the temple was a place of gloom and doom. The passages of human suffering at God's hands and his wrath intrigue us and draw our attention. However, joy, festivity and celebration were integral parts of life in his Presence. God was their delight!

God instructed Israel to observe three festivals each year, all of which were to last seven days and take place in front of the tabernacle: the festival of unleavened bread, the festival of first fruits, and the feast of booths (Hebrew word for a small hut or dwelling). Each celebration was a time of thanksgiving, singing, and dancing before the Lord. Even the daily offerings at the tabernacle were occasions of joy and delight for the Lord's goodness and faithfulness. And as we have already noted, when the Ark of the Covenant was placed in the permanent temple built by Solomon, worship and praise were offered in the Presence continually by hundreds of singers and musicians.

5. From the Ark, he established his mystery and uniqueness.

A man named Rudolph Otto coined a term for the Presence. He called it the "mysterium tremendum," simply translated "awful mystery."[2] R. C. Sproul, in talking about Otto's remark, says that we feel much the same way about the Presence as we do about ghost stories and horror movies. "[W]e are at the same time attracted to it and repulsed by it. Something draws us toward it while at the same time we want to run away from it."[3] The Athanasian Creed simply says, "God is incomprehensible."

The Ark of the Covenant supported this assessment. Hidden behind the veil in the Holy of Holies, it was both intriguing and frightening. The Israelites guarded it day and night, yet only the priests would go near it. The tabernacle was shrouded in mystery and surrounded by a sense of wonderment.

Part of the mystery of the Ark can be attributed to the stark contrast between the two paternal sides of God that emanated from it toward his own children—his extravagant love and provision and his staggeringly harsh discipline. For example, when the Philistines returned the Ark to the Israelites in the town of Beth Shemesh, the people immediately gathered around it to offer sacrifices, rejoicing and celebrating. It was a happy time. But as the celebration started to wind down, things took a dramatic turn. The Lord "struck down some of the men of Beth Shemesh, putting seventy of them to death because they had looked into the ark..." (1 Samuel 6:19). It seems like a rather dismal way to end a party.

But that was God—wholly good and full of blessing, yet quick to bring down the hatchet the instant a line was crossed. It made him seem all the more intriguing. "Come," the Presence seemed to say, "and take delight in me. But don't ever forget who I am—not even for a moment."

The mystery of the Presence beckons people to seek the invisible God. It invites them to yearn for more and more of him. Oh, to go behind the veil! Yet it is only by revelation that we can know and experience him. He must reveal himself to us, and for the Israelites, this revelation came in the tabernacle. It was not just an intellectual head trip, but a spiritual encounter of the most humbling kind. When God revealed himself, people fell to their faces. It seemed an automatic response to his majesty. The veil was necessary to cover the sheer energy of his being lest his glory consume the whole earth.

"Come," the Presence seemed to say, "and take delight in me. But don't ever forget who I am—not even for a moment."

Never in the history of the world has there ever been or will there ever be a god like Jehovah. A divine mystery, he is totally unique. He defies our most creative explanations and our most scientific ideas.

Moses put it this way:

Ask now about the former days, long before your time, from the day God created man on the earth; ask from one end of the heavens to the other. Has anything so great as this ever happened, or has anything like it ever been heard of? Has any other people heard the voice of God speaking out of fire, as you have, and lived? Has any god ever tried to take for himself one nation out of another nation, by testing, by miraculous signs and wonders, by war, by a mighty hand and an outstretched arm, or by great and awesome deeds, like all the things the LORD your God did for you in Egypt before your very eyes?

You were shown these things so that you might know that the LORD is God; besides him there is no other.

Acknowledge and take to heart this day that the LORD is God in heaven above and on the earth below. There is no other (Deuteronomy 4:32-35, 39).

Consider this. The owner of the universe, creator of the galaxies and everything beyond, the God who exists eternally without change decides to reveal himself on the earth. So where does he choose to appear? The Biltmore Mansion? The Luxembourg Castle? St. Peter's Basilica? No. He makes his entrance in a portable tent atop a wooden box among nomadic people who own nothing. Today, this would be the equivalent of him appearing in a Winnebago atop a box of mesquite wood with a group of transients traveling through west Texas.

God didn't choose for his people the great Aztec race, the staff at Microsoft or the Joint Chiefs of Staff. He chose uneducated slaves, said, "Come with me," and then made Pharaoh get out of the way. He brought them out to call them his own treasured possession. He loved them with an everlasting, even jealous love that looked beyond their imperfections. He gave them his name and made covenant with them.

What does all of this say to us? Maybe it should make us rethink our ideas about cathedrals and thrones. Perhaps it should cause us to consider the mind-boggling oxymoron that Philip Yancey calls a "humble God." We might even need to reevaluate the myriad rituals we have that we believe attract his Presence.

Truly, God's ways are not our ways, and his thoughts are not our thoughts! (Isaiah 55:8)

6. From the Ark, he offered atonement for sin.

By the days of Moses and the Israelites, the time of intimacy that Adam and Eve had experienced with God in the Garden was long gone. The sin nature had taken charge and charged more than we could ever pay. Rebellion, hate and shame were born and multiplied as the human race traded security for insecurity. Man was separated from God and hopelessly out of control.

Yet God ached in love to return his creation to a place of communion with him. Therefore, he embarked on a series of covenants with man designed to bring them back into relationship. From the Mercy Seat on the Ark of the Covenant, God, in his compassion, would offer man a remedy for his sin and unrighteousness. Just as the Mercy Seat covered the Law (Ten Commandments) contained in the Ark, so the Presence would cover man's inability to keep the law. The Presence offered man the option of choosing grace over judgment, life over death (Deuteronomy 30:19).

Through God's own self-disclosure in Exodus 34:6-7, we

know that he defines himself as one who forgives "wickedness, rebellion and sin." The Hebrew word for "forgive" in this passage means to "lift up, carry off, or take away." Here in the Holy of Holies, from between the two cherubim, the Presence of God would lift up, carry off and take away the sins of his people. Here, at the Ark, they could find pardon and cleansing. Iniquity could be eradicated. Even when they rebelled and doubted God, he would not stay angry because he delights in showing mercy (Micah 7:18).

Of course, a blood payment still had to be made for sin, and that payment was made by the priests in the form of a sacrifice on the Seat of Atonement once a year. If the offering was acceptable, the Presence would descend in fire and consume it, and mercy would shine from between the angels. Although this arrangement provided only temporary relief for mankind, it foretold of the greatest sacrifice that was to come later.

The goal of atonement was to make the race holy again, as God had intended. "...[B]e holy because I, the LORD your God, am holy" (Leviticus 11:44; 19:2; 20:7-26). God's idea of "holy" here was not absolute purity or perfection; he knew that man could never achieve that on his own. By "holy" he meant "separated, set apart, or consecrated." By his own choosing, he would make his people holy and pleasing in his sight.

> And the LORD has declared this day that you are his
> people, his treasured possession as he promised, and
> that you are to keep all his commands. He has de-
> clared that he will set you in praise, fame and honor

high above all the nations he has made and that you
will be a people holy to the LORD your God, as he
promised (Deuteronomy 26:18-19).

Through atonement for sin, the Israelites would not only
bear God's name, but his glory as well. He wanted his people to
be bent on doing his will, not their own. He wanted love to have
its way on earth as it is in heaven. In the people he called his
treasured possession, he would display his splendor and majesty
for the world to see.

The Covenant

Every dealing God had with his people from the Mercy
Seat was spelled out in the covenant he made with Moses—one
of the series of such covenants that God entered into with Noah,
Abraham, Moses and David in order to restore his original "Garden of Eden" intent by redeeming mankind. The covenant was
the legal agreement ratified in heaven that bound the two parties
to certain relational rules. This is important to keep in mind because on no occasion did God ever act randomly or arbitrarily.
Even his actions that seem difficult to understand or explain were
in line with the covenant to which he had pledged himself.

God, of course, always upheld his end of the covenant
completely and without flaw. The Israelites, on the other hand,
seemed to be doing good to keep their end of the deal for two
days in a row. Because the covenant was only binding and good
if both sides kept it, God ultimately had to enter the earth through
Jesus and keep our side for us. It was through Jesus' sinless life

and death that the covenant was finally sealed and the eternal separation between God and man was abolished once and for all. There would never be a need for another covenant

The Ark was a symbol of the covenant—a reminder to the Israelites of both the boundaries and the benefits of a relationship with the Alpha and Omega, Creator of the universe. It was God's throne, an introduction to his kingdom on earth. Today, we have a different symbol of the covenant through which we are redeemed—a new "Ark." His name is Jesus.

Discussion Questions

1. What three things were contained in the Ark of the Covenant and what did each represent?

2. God didn't like it when the Israelites questioned the authority he had granted to Moses and other appointed leaders. In light of this, discuss how pastors are treated today and how you think it affects the church.

3. Why do you think God was so specific in his instructions regarding the Ark, the tabernacle, the priestly garments, etc.?

4. What does it mean to be "holy."

5. What was the Ark a symbol of?

6. If you could choose, would you relate to God like:

> Moses - face to face
>
> The Levites - dangerously close to the flame
>
> The Israelites - happy to watch from a distance

JESUS
THE NEW ARK

The Ark of the Covenant in the tabernacle was wonderful, but it was not God's last, best word about his Presence on earth. For one thing, it was localized. The Presence was confined to the Ark in the Holy of Holies, which worked out pretty well for the Israelites but didn't do much for the other people groups in the world. Also, God's Presence in the Old Testament was easily mishandled, as we have already seen, often with terrifying results. The raw, unbridled awesomeness of God's being was simply too dangerous for man to deal with. Only Moses and a select few could get close.

Another problem is that God's Presence on the Ark was impersonal. While it enabled God to be experienced and heard by his chosen people through a small group of consecrated priests, it did not allow him intimate contact with each and every individual as he desires. Finally, because the Presence rested on the Ark of the Covenant, the people found it all too easy to enshrine the box itself. They would shift the focus of their worship and trust from the intangible God to the tangible Ark, so mysterious and powerful in their midst.

In short, the Presence was available, but access was very limited. The Ark, as magnificent as it was, was only a prototype of what would follow. "The law is only a shadow of the good things that are coming—not the realities themselves" (Hebrews 10:1). In other words, the law was just a temporary fix that foretold the reality of the consummation of the Presence in the person of Jesus Christ.

On Christmas Day, the new Ark was born into the earth in a manger in the city of Bethlehem. As shepherds held the baby Jesus, they held the Presence of God in human form. The same God that rested on the Mercy Seat in the tabernacle and revealed himself through clouds, fire and miraculous signs entered the earth once again as a tiny helpless infant. And they called him Emmanuel, "God with us" (Matthew 1:23).

Jesus would become the new Ark—the forever resting place of God's Presence. He would put into effect a new Covenant that would remedy all the shortcomings of every covenant that had gone before. Jesus was the pinnacle in the sequence of God's plan to reconnect with the people he created and loved so much. He would take the Presence to a new level of experience and revelation.

John described Jesus' advent to earth in tabernacle language when he said, "The Word became flesh and made his dwelling among us. We have seen his glory, the glory of the One and Only, who came from the Father, full of grace and truth" (John 1:14). The Greek word for "dwelling" in this passage also means "to live in a tabernacle or tent." Jesus "tabernacled" among us. In Jesus, the Presence in every tense would be known: the God of Abraham and Moses who was before the world existed, God fully present now manifested in signs and wonders, and the gift of eternal life made available for every heart (John 6:40).

There were other vestiges of Old Testament scenes in Jesus' life. For example, Jesus often went up on a mountainside to pray, reminiscent of Moses' mountainside visits with God in the desert. Also, the description of Jesus' baptism by the Holy Spirit sounds very similar to some of the early scenes in Israel's camp when God's Presence would descend on the tabernacle:

> And as he was praying, heaven was opened and the Holy Spirit descended on him in bodily form like a dove. And a voice came from heaven: "You are my Son, whom I love; with you I am well pleased" (Luke 3:21-22).

In addition, consider the following passages:

> ...but stay in the city until you have been *clothed with power from on high* (Luke 24:49).

> After he said this, he was taken up before their very eyes, and *a cloud hid him* from their sight (Acts 1:9).

Suddenly a *sound like the blowing of a violent wind* came from heaven and *filled the whole house* where they were sitting. They saw what seemed to be *tongues of fire* that separated and came to rest on each of them (Acts 2:2-3).

The Presence was still a supernatural force to be reckoned with; however in Jesus it exerted its power through a humble spirit and wise, gentle words.

The veil around the Holy of Holies would be rent forever and replaced with a welcome mat, "Remain in me."

In the new Ark, clouds would no longer be needed. One could look into his eyes and even touch his face and not die. Fire would still be his trademark, but now it would burn in the spirits of those who believed (Luke 24:32). In Jesus, the Presence would become accessible to anyone who drew near; it would no longer be dangerous or confined to the shores of the Mediterranean Sea. The veil around the Holy of Holies would be rent forever and replaced with a welcome mat, "Remain in me" (John 15:1-17). God would reveal himself through the Son in new dimensions of love, compassion and restraint.

Sally Morgenthaler says:

Jesus Christ is *how* we know God. But, even more

importantly, Jesus Christ is the only way we *access* God. We have confidence to 'enter the Most Holy Place' only by 'the blood of Jesus, by a new and living way opened for us through the curtain, that is, his body' (Heb. 10:19-20). Thus Christian worship happens only through Jesus.[1]

Purposes Fulfilled in Jesus

As the new Ark, Jesus in the New Testament fulfilled the same purposes that were fulfilled by the Ark in the Old Testament—not in the prophetic sense of fulfillment, but in function. The Presence characteristics remained consistent throughout the Bible since God's nature is unchanging and Jesus preexisted with him before time began. Jesus prayed, "And now, Father, glorify me in your presence with the glory I had with you before the world began" (John 17:5). His DNA was made of eternal stuff.

It is important to see these consistencies because we need to understand that the Presence of God has not changed and will never change. Only the benchmark on which he rests, or the manner in which he reveals himself will ever change. All cities have a benchmark. Railroads have a benchmark. The benchmark is the point from which all other objects are aligned, and the Presence of God as revealed in the person of Jesus is now our benchmark as Christians. The plumb line points to him.

Jesus is the starting point to which everything else must relate. Just as the Israelites placed the Ark in the very center of their camp, Jesus must be the central focal point for Presence based thinking and worship because everything about God is seen in the Son. "Anyone who has seen me has seen the Father" (John 14:9). To be Presence based is to be Christocentric.

1. In Jesus, God displayed his power and authority.

God's power and authority were quite evident in the life of Jesus. Wherever he went he unequivocally answered the question, "Who's in charge here?" Just as God told Moses to tell the people, "I AM has sent me to you" (Exodus 3:14), Jesus reiterated his Father's words often and with the same divine confidence. The Greek is very explicit, "Ego Emi," I AM.

Jesus said:

I am the bread of life (John 6:35, 41, 48, 51).

I am the light of the world (John 8:12, 16, 18).

I am from above. I am not from this world (John 8:23, 28).

…before Abraham was born, *I am*! (John 8:58)

I am the gate for the sheep (John 10:7, 9).

I am the good shepherd (John 10:11, 14).

I am the resurrection and the life (John 11:25).

I am the way and the truth and the life (John 14:6).

Many references in John's gospel alone declare Jesus as the "I AM"—the very essence of the Presence. And just as it was in the Old Testament, "I AM" was a very powerful declaration of God's independent status and authority over the human race, even in the person of Jesus.

For example, when the religious leaders found Jesus in the

Garden to arrest him, he said simply, "I am he," and the whole bunch fell to the ground (John 18:6). What's amazing is that they arrested him anyway! I believe I would have paused to reflect for a moment before putting a man with that kind of supernatural power in handcuffs.

God's power and authority were so evident in Jesus' life that his very presence on the scene tormented the religious leaders of the day. He was there to establish a higher rule and reign than theirs, and they knew it. They wanted to be in charge, but they recognized in Jesus a level of authority that was above all and rooted in something much bigger than their laws and customs.

Even the people, as Matthew observed, recognized the difference between authority given by God and authority fabricated by man, "When Jesus had finished saying these things, the crowds were amazed at his teaching, because he taught as one who had authority, and not as their teachers of the law" (Matthew 7:29). Ouch! No wonder the religious teachers were uncomfortable with Jesus. It was obvious that he was different.

It is interesting that in Matthew, Mark and Luke, Jesus cast out demons. But in the book of John, he confronted the Pharisees and Sadducees. It was these religious leaders that finally crucified Jesus in an attempt to maintain control and satisfy their jealous designs. He threatened everything they had worked for.

We can learn a great deal from the way Jesus responded to criticism and even hostility. He had an interesting method of conflict management. For example, when Jesus visited his home town of Nazareth, the people became so angry that he would not perform any miracles there, that they physically drove him out of town to a hilltop with the intention of throwing him down the cliff. But before they could act, Jesus "walked right through the crowd and went on his way" (Luke 4:30). I just love that. The Presence can not be contained by man.

At another time, Jesus was talking to a group of Jews who became so enraged by his claims that they picked up rocks to stone him. Jesus' response? He "hid himself, slipping away from the temple grounds" (John 8:59). And when Jesus was brought before Pilate, the elders, and the Sanhedrin as they made their case to crucify him, he stood silent. Pilate asked him, "'Aren't you going to answer? See how many things they are accusing you of?' But Jesus still made no reply, and Pilate was amazed" (Mark 15:3-5).

When the heat was on, Jesus got very quiet. He didn't do a lot of arguing. Instead, he let the Presence that was so evident in his life speak for itself. The Presence was his justification and his answer. It was his authority. He didn't need to prove that he was right because he was Truth personified, blameless and above reproach. I wonder how the church would be different today if we adopted Jesus' confrontation strategy? Would the Presence of God be evident enough to speak if we were silent?

We often hear it said that a leader is effective because he or she has "presence." However, in the Bible, leaders were ordained by *the* Presence, which is why so many unlikely candidates became heroes in the kingdom. Jesus had no credentials of the day— no seminary education, no formal religious training, no books to his name and no weekly radio program. But he bore the impri-

matur of God, and that put him in a class by himself. "All authority in heaven and on earth has been given to me," he said (Matthew 28:18).

In addition to having Presence to govern, Jesus picked up
where the Father left off in the business of supernatural signs
and wonders. Throughout his ministry, Jesus demonstrated God's
power over the natural universe through a wide variety of miracles.
In the Old Testament, God turned the Nile River into blood as a
sign to Pharaoh (Exodus 7:17). In the New Testament, Jesus
turned water into wine at a wedding party (John 2:1-11). God
parted the Red Sea to let the Israelites pass through (Exodus 14).
Jesus calmed the winds and the waves so that his disciples would
not be afraid (Matthew 8:26-27). God provided manna from
heaven for the Israelites to eat (Exodus 16:4). Jesus fed a crowd
of 5,000 people from a few fish and loaves of bread (Matthew
14:13-21). Like Father, like Son. He even encouraged skeptics to
take note of the miracles as evidence of his own authenticity,
"But if I do it, even though you do not believe me, believe the
miracles, that you may know and understand that the Father is in
me, and I in the Father" (John 10:38).

The power that flowed through Jesus was like quintessential energy that was always available. The woman in the crowd
who had been suffering in her body for many years tapped into
that power source when she reached out and touched Jesus'
clothes. "At once Jesus realized that power had gone out from
him. He turned around in the crowd and asked, 'Who touched
my clothes?'" (Mark 5:30) Jesus operated in the power of the

Spirit (Luke 4:14) to heal and set captives free (Luke 4:40-41; 5:17).

2. Through Jesus, God communicated his will to us.

After the Ark disappeared, the world suffered through 400 or more years of silence on God's part until he again stepped through the veil into the natural realm in the person of Jesus. And for another brief period in history, God spoke very directly to his people. But this time around there were no clouds or fire, no terrifying special effects, just the Messiah in a boat, on a hill, or walking through the streets surrounded by people, talking and teaching about the kingdom of God.

Just as God had in the Old Testament, Jesus had a lot to say. Through sermons and parables, private conversations and public speaking opportunities, he taught about his mission, the end times, salvation, forgiveness, family life, church life, prayer and heaven. It is little wonder that in the New Testament the only audible words we hear from the Father are, "This is my Son, whom I love; with him I am well pleased. Listen to him!" (Matthew 17:5; Luke 3:22)

Jesus made the voice of his Father tender and gentle and available to all. He explained, "My teaching is not my own. It comes from him who sent me" (John 7:16). His message was of a New Covenant, one he had come to fulfill. He spoke of a new hope, a new way and a new life through him. His words were given to guide and govern life on earth until he comes again in full glory to establish his kingdom here once and for all.

One of the most significant things Jesus did by carrying out the Father's plan for redemption was to become our passageway into the Holy Presence. Yes, he communicated rules for healthy living and secrets for abundant life, but perhaps more significantly he made it possible for *every* person to communicate personally and intimately back to God. He opened the door to the Holy of Holies and made it safe for us to go in. He gave himself on the altar as the one, perfect atoning sacrifice, and in doing so, he completely redefined the concept of prayer.

But this time around there were no clouds or fire..., just the Messiah in a boat, on a hill, or walking through the streets...

A good three-fourths of the references to prayer in the Bible are found in the New Testament. And it's no wonder, since Jesus modeled a life of prayer (Mark 1:35) and taught us Prayer 101 (Matthew 6:5-13). He revealed that prayer was not only safe; it was our lifeline to the Presence. In him we could talk directly to God and actually hear him answer. It was our own personal connection to the Father, a workable stand-in to the one that had been so grievously lost in the Garden of Eden when sin demanded our separation.

Now in prayer, we could know the Father's heart and will. We could hear his voice. We could sense his Presence. Through the lifeline of prayer, God could once again reveal himself to us and bestow on us the mind of Christ.

In addition to giving us access to the inner sanctuary of

God's Presence, Jesus pointed us to the Holy Spirit who would come to reside in us and guide us when he returned to the Father. The Holy Spirit would be the Presence in us, and would become the new voice of God, communicating with every believer and empowering us from within for the work of ministry. "But when he, the Spirit of truth, comes, he will guide you into all truth. He will not speak on his own; he will speak only what he hears, and he will tell you what is yet to come" (John 16:13).

God never again wanted to be without a way to communicate with his children. "Whoever believes in me, as the Scripture has said, streams of living water will flow from within him" (John 7:38). Then John goes on to explain that by "streams of living water," Jesus was referring to the Holy Spirit, "whom those who believed in him were later to receive" (John 7:39). In the same manner that God used the cloud to tell the Israelites when to move and when to camp, he sent us the Holy Spirit to give us direction according to his will and purpose.

3. In Jesus, God gave us victory over our enemies.

Evil has never fared well in the Presence. Perfect in love and holiness, God's matchless dominion snuffs out or crumbles any representation of evil that comes near. Just as the statue of Dagon fell to the ground and was decapitated in submission to the true living God, evil has no other alternatives in the Presence than to bow, flee or face destruction.

The Presence of God was so real in Jesus that "whenever the evil spirits saw him, they fell down before him and cried out, 'You are the Son of God'" (Mark 3:11). On several occasions,

Jesus exercised his authority over Satan and his demons by driving them out and sending them away (Mark 5:1-13; Luke 9:37-45).

Although Satan still has freedom to participate in the cosmic battle for souls, he knows his time is limited. The outcome has already been predestined and he is the eternal loser. Jesus' death on the cross and subsequent resurrection to life sent shockwaves through the spiritual realm and sealed Satan's fate with absolute finality. Our fate, too, turned dramatically on that singular, magnificent moment in the history of the world when life began to pulse anew through Jesus' decaying body as he lay in the tomb. In that divinely orchestrated instant, all the rules changed. At that one moment—when Jesus drew breath again into his lungs and his heart muscle pushed blood back into his veins and his wounded and bruised body was instantly restored to wholeness except the beautiful telltale scars—at that moment, the victory was won.

In that divinely orchestrated instant, all the rules changed.

"And having disarmed the powers and authorities, he made a public spectacle of them, triumphing over them by the cross" (Colossians 2:15). The Presence in the Old Testament contained evil; Jesus defeated evil to the point of humiliation! Now those of us who are in Christ as believers have the power of attorney to exercise his authority on the earth.

A college student named Sabrina that attended my church

years ago experienced the power Jesus' name has over the enemy. She was awakened one night by the sound of an intruder in her apartment. Frightened, she lay motionless until the man approached her bed and started pulling on the sheet. Suddenly, she sat up and screamed, "In the name of Jesus, you get out of here now!" The would-be assailant almost stumbled to the floor trying to get out of the patio door. Although we don't carry a wooden chest, we do carry the essence of the Presence when we speak the name of Jesus in boldness and faith.

The Israelites carried the Ark of God's Presence into battle before them because they depended on God to give them victory. Now Jesus is the Ark of God's Presence and it is he whom we lift up in the face of evil. He is our refuge and stronghold when the enemy attacks. John wrote, "You, dear children, are from God and have overcome them, because the one who is in you is greater than the one who is in the world" (1 John 4:4).

Since Jesus ascended into heaven, he left us his name to be our access to the power of his resurrection. He gave us power of attorney to be his representatives until he returns. The name "Jesus" falls on Satan's ears like fingernails on a chalkboard, because it unleashes the full effect of the cross like a laser at the point of kingdom conflict. Paul writes:

> Therefore God exalted him to the highest place and gave him the name that is above every name, that at the name of Jesus every knee should bow in heaven and on earth and under the earth, and every tongue confess that Jesus Christ is Lord, to the glory of God

the Father (Philippians 2:9-11).

In essence, to do spiritual warfare we simply invoke or welcome the Presence of God and all evil retreats as we worship and delight in him. We don't have to give Satan undue attention. We give God our allegiance in a salute of praise, and evil bows.

4. Through Jesus, God demonstrated his favor and delight toward us.

When the Presence of God returned to the earth in Jesus, the earth-shaking, fire-breathing God of the Israelites had redressed himself as a mild-mannered carpenter, the "Good Shepherd." It wasn't that God's character had changed. He was the same Jehovah. But it was time for the world to "grasp how wide and long and high and deep is the love of Christ, and to know this love that surpasses knowledge—that you may be filled to the measure of all the fullness of God" (Ephesians 3:18-19). This time around, God was on a mission of grace and mercy.

Jesus was the perfect personification of God's favor, love, delight and affection for us. He called himself a bridegroom, and called us his bride (Isaiah 62:5; Revelation 19:7). How much more could he say about his devotion to us? Nothing compares to the feelings of passion and delight of a young couple on their wedding day. As the bride of Christ, we are loved, pursued, desired and enjoyed. The prophet says:

> On that day they will say to Jerusalem, "Do not fear,
> O Zion; do not let your hands hang limp. The LORD
> your God is with you, he is mighty to save. He will
> take great delight in you, he will quiet you with his

love, he will rejoice over you with singing"
(Zephaniah 3:16-17).

As I mentioned before, I believe God smiles at us, much like a father might smile watching his son playing with a new puppy or trying to catch a frog. Regardless of what is going on in my adult world, I can't help but smile when I see one of my grandchildren because they are innately precious to me. They can be dirty from head to toe or trying their mother's patience with any number of misbehaviors—it doesn't matter. They know they have my favor because my face lights up every time they walk in the door!

God's favor toward us radiated from the face of Jesus, and his smile penetrated all sorts of human conditions. In him, we can sense the favor of God's smile even when our life is messy or we're misbehaving. Jesus' life demonstrated that the Father's favor is not dependent on us, but is a godly attribute given to us when we exchange his life for ours. If we had to attain the favor of God, we would never be able to do it.

Because of the Father's great love for us, he sent his Son to give and to bless. God is good and God is love. He can be no other way. He lavishes upon us all sorts of blessings in accordance with his will and purpose. "From the fullness of his grace we have all received one blessing after another. For the law was given through Moses; grace and truth came through Jesus Christ" (John 1:16-17). God's smile was never bigger than it was in the Son.

Adam and Eve lived in God's benevolence before they stumbled and fell. Jesus came to pick us up and pull us back into the lap of God's enduring grace. "And I will do whatever you ask in my name, so that the Son may bring glory to the Father. You may ask me for anything in my name, and I will do it" (John 14:13-14).

Consider all the things that Jesus came to give:

He gave time.

He gave hope.

He gave acceptance.

He gave blessing.

He gave a mission.

He gave life.

He gave comfort.

He gave peace.

He gave the Holy Spirit.

He gave joy.

He gave a new kingdom.

He gave protection.

He gave giving.

He gave healing.

He gave deliverance.

He gave prayer.

He gave unity.

He gave love.

He gave vision.

He gave victory.

He gave miracles.

Most importantly, he gave us the privilege of living in the Presence.

Jesus was an amazingly generous person for a man who never owned anything. As a result, his Presence fosters an atmosphere of blessing. The New Covenant that he ratified on the cross meant that all that was his was ours, and all that was ours was his.

God created us to be his delight, and he desired that we also delight in him. His Presence is to be our joy (Psalm 21:6). Jesus came so that we might experience the full measure of his joy here and now, and in heaven (John 16:24; 17:13). Nothing compares to the delight of knowing God's Presence.

5. In Jesus, God confirmed his mystery and uniqueness.

The God who showed up in the Old Testament on a wooden box in the desert among nomadic slaves made an equally unique entrance into the earth the second time—a baby, conceived out of wedlock to a teenage girl and a blue collar laborer, born in a stable in a tiny town in the middle of the night. His reputation was tarnished before he even was delivered. "Bastard" children in those days did not have the same privileges as legitimate children, nor did they have legal claim to paternal care. And imagine what Mary's friends and family (not to mention her youth leader!) must have thought.

Jesus' lineage was questionable as well: Ruth a Moabite, Rahab a Canaanite prostitute, David an adulterer and murderer, and Solomon who had more wives than Larry King. The only people who showed up to celebrate the newborn baby were shepherds—no Jerusalem press corps and no dignitaries.

No wonder Paul wrote about Jesus:

Who, being in very nature God, did not consider equality with God something to be grasped, but *made himself nothing*, taking the very nature of a servant, being made in human likeness. And being found in appearance as a man, he humbled himself and became obedient to death—even death on a cross (Philippians 2:6-8, italics mine).

Another version reads that he "became of no reputation."

Philip Yancey describes God's unlikely appearance like this:

Unimaginably, the Maker of all things shrank down, down, down, so small as to become an ovum, a single fertilized egg barely visible to the naked eye, an egg that would divide and redivide until a fetus took shape, enlarging cell by cell inside a nervous teenager. "Immensity cloistered in thy dear womb," marveled the poet John Donne.

The God who roared, who could order armies and empires around like pawns on a chessboard, this God emerged in Palestine as a baby who could not speak or eat solid food or control his bladder, who depended on a teenager for shelter, food and love.[2]

I try to wrap my mind around the creator of the universe coming in this manner, but the whole idea is really absurd. Every time I think about it, I just have to marvel at the irony of the King of all kings in diapers. El Shaddai, "the breasted one," would now be breastfed by a young mother.

Consider the manner in which earthly dignitaries present themselves—fancy cars, expensive attire, numerous attendants and bodyguards, and big fanfare. They stay in five-star hotels and mingle with the wealthy and influential. These are the images we associate with glory and honor.

From the Ark in the desert to the stable in Bethlehem, he owned nothing and lived among the poorest, nameless people in society.

Not so with Jehovah. He always chose the most humble, unassuming ways. In fact, humility was his trademark. From the Ark in the desert to the stable in Bethlehem, he owned nothing and lived among the poorest, nameless people in society. He made his one "triumphal" entry into Jerusalem on a borrowed donkey, and culminated his life's mission by subjecting himself to a criminal's death on a wooden cross. What kind of king has ever been like Jesus?

Yet King he was. Paul wrote:

He is the image of the invisible God, the firstborn over all creation. He is before all things, and in him all things hold together. For God was pleased to have all his fullness dwell in him.... For in Christ all the fullness of the Deity lives in bodily form..." (Colossians 1:15, 17, 19; 2:9).

The uniqueness of Jesus' birth made the mystery that surrounded him even greater.

In Solomon's temple a thick, heavy curtain or veil surrounded the Holy of Holies, concealing The Ark of the Covenant, the mystery of godliness. Words like fascination, intrigue, wonder and fear surrounded the gold seat that held God's Presence. Behind the veil was the great "I AM."

When Jesus died on the cross, that veil in the temple was ripped in two from top to bottom (Matthew 27:51). It was God's way of saying that the door had been opened to his Presence. The veil no longer concealed it. Now, in Jesus, anyone could enter the Holy of Holies to know and experience God in a personal way.

The mystery of God, however, was not completely revealed in Jesus. In fact, God in human form so transcends our sensory perception that it almost stacks mystery upon mystery. The mystery of God is a constant in the spiritual world and will remain so until we get to heaven. Until that time, we will never fully understand him. But Jesus provided us a way to at least begin the journey of discovering and unpacking the magnitude of God. It is called the revelation of Jesus.

God is infinitely deep and exciting and profound, so much so that all the books in the world wouldn't amount to an anthill compared to the mountain of what there is to know about God. Yet by the revelation of Jesus, we have a graceful ladder on which to start the ascent.

We can only know God to the extent that Jesus reveals him to us. It is not the kind of knowledge we can find in a book or even gain with age or experience. It can not be earned—it must be given by God himself. Even the disciples couldn't "figure Jesus out" on their own. When Jesus asked Simon Peter, "Who do you say I am?" Simon Peter replied, "You are the Christ, the Son of the living God." Then Jesus told Peter, "Blessed are you, Simon son of Jonah, for this was not revealed to you by man, but by my Father in heaven" (Matthew 16:15-17).

The revelation of Jesus is given at the sovereign decision of the Creator. The moment was so significant to Jesus that he went on to tell the disciples not to tell anyone who he was, because others too would have to receive the revelation from the Father for themselves.

Peter would go on to write in his own epistle, "Therefore, gird up your minds; be sober; set your hope fully upon the grace that is coming to you at the revelation of Jesus Christ" (1 Peter 1:13, RSV). In other words, don't stop at just seeing Jesus as savior and provider. Press on to know him deeper, to be caught up in his revelation.

Perhaps the greatest revelation of Jesus was made known to John on the isle of Patmos. His entire letter—the book of Revelation—is his attempt to explain what he heard and saw.

The revelation of Jesus is a layer by layer unfolding of divine secrets to those with one common attribute—hunger. Age doesn't matter, education doesn't matter, and social status or race doesn't matter. God gives himself in response to one thing and one thing only, and that is the burning desire to know him. A poverty stricken woman in a hut in Africa can experience the revelation of Jesus just as easily as a respected theologian in North America. Perhaps easier. She better understands what it means to be truly hungry.

God gives himself in response to one thing and one thing only, and that is the burning desire to know him.

When once we begin to experience the revelation of Jesus, we will be swept away by his beauty and wonder, and at the same time brought to our knees in overwhelming humility. He becomes more infinite and we become more finite. He catches us up like a kite in a hurricane.

6. Through Jesus, God offered atonement for sin.

As mentioned before, the Ark of the Covenant represented a promise—a covenant—between God and his chosen people. But in order for the covenant to be binding, both parties had to keep the agreement. If either failed to do so, the covenant would be broken.

A quick read through Exodus will tell you that the Israelites broke the rules, the Ten Commandments contained in the Ark, more often than a four month old puppy. The people were plagued with *sin*—their state of separation from God incurred in the Garden, and with *sins*—the things they did wrong every day.

The only way for them to restore their relationship to God was through blood sacrifice of an unblemished lamb. "In fact, the law requires that nearly everything be cleansed with blood, and without the shedding of blood there is no forgiveness" (Hebrews 9:22). Thus, the priests went in once a year and offered the sacrifice on the Mercy Seat. In doing so, they restored fellowship with God, even if temporarily. Sadly, the process had to be repeated over and over, and their precious times of relief and forgiveness in the Presence never lasted. "...[I]t can never, by the same sacrifices repeated endlessly year after year, make perfect those who draw near to worship" (Hebrews 10:1). The Israelites could visit in the Presence, but they couldn't stay.

When Jesus entered the picture, fully God yet fully man, he did what no man could ever do—he kept every commandment. He walked out a life here on earth sinless and blameless in every regard. He did not break a single law of God or man, even in his heart. Jesus kept the covenant for all of us so that he could put in place a new covenant that would allow us to come freely into the Presence and remain there.

Holy and pure, Jesus became the final atoning sacrifice. Jesus laid his body down, the eternal unblemished lamb, as payment for all the sin in the world, both past and future. His blood became the atoning blood in which all mankind could find forgiveness and redemption. No more sacrifice would be needed because in God's plan, the blood of Jesus covered everything. The Old Testament payment plan was over and the coupon book was thrown away!

> For Christ did not enter a manmade sanctuary that
> was only a copy of the true one; he entered heaven
> itself, now to appear for us in God's presence. Nor

did he enter heaven to offer himself again and again, the way the high priest enters the Most Holy Place every year with blood that is not his own. Then Christ would have had to suffer many times since the creation of the world. But now he has appeared once for all at the end of the ages to do away with sin by the sacrifice of himself (Hebrews 9:24-26).

Recall that the Hebrew word for "ark" can also be translated as "coffin." Could it be that the Ark of the Covenant foretold of the death of One who would fulfill the Law contained in it? Perhaps the Ark pointed to the cross.

The New Race of the Presence

Jesus opened up the Presence of God for us to enjoy and abide in for eternity. The only requirement would be the acceptance of his gift of mercy. By faith in Jesus, the Bible says we actually exchange our old life for a new one that is righteous in God's sight. "God made him who had no sin to be sin for us, so that in him we might become the righteousness of God" (2 Corinthians 5:21). "Therefore, if anyone is in Christ, he is a new creation; the old has gone, the new has come!" (2 Corinthians 5:17)

It is interesting that the Greek for "new creation" also means "new race." Jesus actually came to create a new race of Presence-bound, God pleasing people who would display his glory and splendor. Peter sums it up:

But you are a chosen people, a royal priesthood, a holy nation, people belonging to God, that you may declare the praises of him who called you out of darkness into his wonderful light. Once you were not a people, but now you are the people of God; once you had not received mercy, but now you have received mercy (1 Peter 2:9-10).

Jesus not only made the Presence accessible to us, he made it possible for God's Presence to live *in* us through the Holy Spirit. Where there once was separation and inevitable death, now there is a union and the promise of eternal life. The law is no longer written in stone, but in the hearts and minds of believers (Hebrews 10:16). We are the new race of the Presence, set apart to receive and reflect his blessings and benefits through the atoning sacrifice of Christ Jesus, the Son. Life is no longer about keeping the rules, but conforming to the image of the Son (Romans 8:29).

If the Ark was God's introduction of his kingdom into the earth, Jesus was the sneak preview. He gave us a glimpse of what God's reign will be like when he returns to judge his creation and establish his kingdom in full once and for all. Jesus spoke often of the kingdom while he was here, as one who knew such a glorious secret that he almost couldn't contain it. He prayed, "Your kingdom come, your will be done on earth as it is in heaven" (Matthew 6:10). He told us to "seek first his kingdom" (Matthew 6:33), and he preached "the good news of the kingdom" (Matthew 9:35). Having come from heaven, he knew what was in store for us and he didn't want anyone to miss out. Jesus became the key, not just to salvation, but to understanding and accessing the Presence in this life.

Discussion Questions

1. Are there objects/rituals/traditions in your church that get more reverence than they deserve?

2. Why was a New Covenant needed?

3. When John the Baptist saw Jesus and said, "Look, the Lamb of God...," what did he mean? (see John 1:29, 35)

4. Why was it necessary for Jesus to live on earth as a man? Why did he have to die?

5. How did Jesus respond when confronted? Why?

6. In light of how the Israelites cared for the Ark, do we as the church treat Jesus as the new resting place of God's Presence?

7. At what moment was evil defeated and our victory secured? Explain.

8. Considering the humility of Moses and Jesus and their corresponding power, what can you conclude about the lack of power in the church?

9. To what extent can we know God? How do we discover him?

10. What role will Jesus play in the Presence based church?

PRESENCE BASED WORSHIP

Remember where we left the Mary church? Rabid about prayer and worship, known by the evidence of the presence of God's power, with the pastor that is a man of God, not of people? As I was saying before our Old Testament expedition, the Mary church is, at its core, what I call a Presence based church. It is part of the new race of God's chosen people, called out of darkness into his light to declare his praise.

Now that we have looked at the Presence of God in the lives of Moses and the Israelites, I can try to bring the Presence based church into focus, for it is best understood against this backdrop. The pattern of relationship between God and man—which started on the Seat of Atonement in the center of Israel's camp and eventually led to Jesus' atoning sacrifice on the cross—this pattern is the foundation of the Presence based church.

First I have to clearly state that the Presence based church is not defined by procedures or specific worship styles. You don't become a Presence based church by following a prescribed formula—singing certain songs, ministering to people in a certain way. Most importantly, a church is not Presence based because of what it does or does not do on Sunday morning. A church service is just the proverbial tip of the iceberg—the weekly expression of all that is going on under the surface.

Over the past decade, as the unity movement has swept across the American church, we have all watched the attributes that once defined "charismatic" and "liturgical" churches, "contemporary" and "traditional" churches become less recognizable due to cross pollination. Walls and barriers between historically segregated styles of worship have become fuzzier and fuzzier until some have become almost invisible. It's no longer easy to identify or label a church based on the form and function of the Sunday morning service. A worshiper today can experience many of the same things in a Baptist church, a community church and an independent church, for example.

I don't think the Christian denominations and traditions will ever completely lose their distinctiveness, nor do I think they necessarily should. But the trend toward embracing similarities and downplaying division has been a breath of fresh air for many churches that have learned from once alienated brothers and sisters. Unity in the body of Christ is essential for two reasons: Without it Christianity will not have any kind of an impact in our spiritually diverse world; and perhaps more importantly, it was

Jesus' prayer for the church.

I say this because I truly believe that *any* church can become more Presence based than it currently is. Any congregation, regardless of size or affiliation, can desire more of God and hunger for his manifest Presence. The issue is not so much about *how* we worship, but *why* we worship, and the heart attitude that we bring to the table.

So what is a Presence based church? What distinguishes it from others if it is not identifiable by its style or activities?

A Heart for Worship

As it was for Moses and the Israelites, the distinguishing mark of the Presence based church is the Ark of God's Presence in the very center of camp. It is a people set apart by the uniquely intimate relationship they have with God, and by the way he reveals himself in their midst. His Presence is their logo, their identity and their source.

With the same enthusiasm that the consumer based church puts into developing and implementing people pleasing programs, the Presence based church devotes itself to creating a God pleasing environment. They want him to come and dwell. That's why worship dominates the Mary church personality. Dick Eastman explains:

> To a degree, I can understand the seeker-sensitive mentality that in some church-growth models intends to create a comfort level for newcomers. Yet, we should not fear a Savior-sensitive worship model ei-

ther, one that seeks to create a climate for the Lord Himself to come—and act! I believe it is possible to have both.[1]

Note that the first commandment God issued to his chosen people dealt with worship: "I am the LORD your God, who brought you out of Egypt, out of the land of slavery. You shall have no other gods before me" (Deuteronomy 5:6-7). Of all the qualities of a Presence based church that I will offer, worship is by far the single most significant, and the one from which the others originate. For that reason, we will look at Presence based worship up front and in depth.

David Watson explains the Presence based church's attitude toward worship in his book, *I Believe in the Church*:

> The primary task of the church is to worship God. Even before the obvious evangelistic and missionary work, God's people are called to be a worshiping community. Having come to Jesus, that "living stone," Christians are to be "like living stones built into a spiritual house." For what purpose? "To be a holy priesthood, to offer spiritual sacrifices acceptable to God through Jesus Christ" (1 Peter 2:9).
>
> Throughout the New Testament the emphasis is the same. "We who first hoped in Christ have been destined and appointed to live for the praise of his glory" (Ephesians 1:12). "Do you not know," asked Paul to the church at Corinth, "that your body is a temple of the Holy Spirit…?" This temple, as all other

temples, is primarily set aside for the worship of God. This is the chief end of man: "to glorify God and to enjoy him forever." [2]

The worship life of the Mary church is driven by an underlying hunger for God's Presence. Like the Israelites who waited in the temple, lured by an intense fascination with the Ark of the Covenant, the people of the Presence based church have tasted the incomparable sweetness of God's nearness and bear his divine imprint. They worship because they are addicted to the Presence of God, and because being created by God for that purpose, they feel more alive and fulfilled during worship than at any other time. It is their passion and joy.

Jack Hayford, chancellor of The King's College and Seminary in Van Nuys, California, writes about what pleases God in worship:

> Ultimately, what is on God's mind when we worship Him is not how many grandiose thoughts we have about Him, but how passionately our hearts desire Him. And what He most wants to achieve in the intercourse of our spirits with His is the transmission of love, life and joy. [3]

The question in the Presence based church is not, "Are we attracting people," but rather, "Are we attracting the Presence of God? Does he feel welcomed and honored above all else?" They live on the cutting edge of worship because they are constantly looking for ways to press beyond any barriers that would hinder their expression of love and adoration.

Recognized globally as a hotbed of innovative worship, New Life Church in Colorado Springs is a Presence based church pushing the edges of worship both corporately and nationally. Pastor Ted Haggard and worship leader Ross Parsley want to increase their investment each year into the worship life not only of their own 15,000 member congregation, but of the body of Christ at large. At the writing of this book, they have recently started the New Life School of Worship, an intensive training program for worship leaders aimed at equipping "worship leaders, singers and instrumentalists with twenty-first century tools and skills to expand the kingdom with confidence and character." The one-year program combines classroom teaching on everything from theology of worship to musical training, with practical experience in the life of a healthy church. (For more information, go to www.newlifeworship.com.)

The question in the Presence based church is not, "Are we attracting people," but rather, "Are we attracting the Presence of God?

New Life Church has been blessed with good worship, but they have a holy discontent that propels them to move forward and reach higher each year. They have set a standard of excellence in worship that is challenging others to do the same.

Tabernacle Worship

As I briefly mentioned earlier, each of the three tabernacles, Moses', David's and Solomon's, seemed to introduce and emphasize a different aspect of worship. The tabernacle of Moses was characterized by waiting and silent worship. The Levites tended to the Presence on the Ark mostly in silence around the clock. Music, liturgies, spoken prayers and sermons were few. They just sat and waited, their attention focused on the tabernacle where the cloud of God would appear.

When he restored the Ark to the tabernacle in Jerusalem, King David introduced praise into the ministry of the Levites. While times of silence were still observed, David's tabernacle became a place of music and singing to the Lord. David wrote Psalms proclaiming the greatness of God and accompanied them with instruments. Sometimes they sang all night, extolling the magnificence of the Presence.

And finally when Solomon built the permanent temple to house the sacred Ark of the Covenant, prayer became a significant part of temple life. Old Testament scholar and author of an exhaustive study of the tabernacles of Moses and David and the temple of Solomon, Kevin Conner explains the significance of Solomon's prayer of dedication found in both 1 Kings 8:12-61 and 2 Chronicles 6:1-42:

> The key words to be noted in these Scriptures have to do with "prayer," "His Name," "this place," "confession of sins," and "this house." The prayer covers every area of personal and national life. This

house was to be a house of prayer for all nations, not just for Israel.[4]

All three of these forms of worship—waiting, praise and prayer—are integral parts of the Presence based church. For example, Pine Castle United Methodist Church in Orlando, Florida is a dynamic growing church that is packed out in two of its three weekend services. Yet Pastor Blake Lorenz is more diligent than ever about welcoming the Presence of God. Every year the church spends the first 10 days of January fervently seeking God in prayer. They come to the sanctuary each night and literally get on their faces before the Lord. They wait, worship and pray for vision and direction. "His Presence is the most important part of our church. We desperately need him," explains Pastor Lorenz.

Another good expression of these various aspects of worship can be seen in local church prayer rooms all across America. Thousands of churches have established rooms dedicated to waiting, praise and prayer, many of them 24-7. There are as many different kinds of prayer rooms as there are churches, but most offer a place of solitude where one can wait on God, enjoy a time of personal worship, or pray through a variety of informative stations. Encouraging churches to build such rooms has been one of the passions of my ministry for over twenty years and is the subject of my book, *Making Room to Pray*.[5]

A pastor named Mike Bickle resigned his role as a senior pastor several years ago to start a city-wide "harp and bowl" center in Kansas City, Missouri. (The harp represents worship and the bowl represents prayer as symbolized in Revelation 5:8b.) The

International House of Prayer, as it is called, is a 24-7 worship and intercession ministry supported and enjoyed by many different churches in that area. They have continuous prayer and praise services throughout the week that last approximately two hours, each one rolling into the next. He explains the power of marrying worship and intercession:

> I speak of intercessory worship because there is an interaction between worship and the speaking of the prayers. Something wonderful happens during the singing of prayers and the speaking of the prayers when the Spirit of God is upon the music. Prayer is easy. And because prayer is easy, people can pray much longer and more often than they could in the past. Prayer becomes refreshing and enjoyable![6]

Since the Presence based church is always looking to push the worship envelope, they like to try different things. They tend to be somewhat creative. The worship leader in a Presence based church may ask that bulletins not be handed out until the end of the service so people won't read during the worship time. He may ask the people to bow or kneel or worship in a prolonged period of silence and listening. He may call for worship vigils or times of extended worship as a church body, and he may introduce his people to worship music from different cultures. Occasionally, he may even dismiss the visitors at the end of the service and invite the regular members to stay and continue worshiping past noon.

One of today's most respected worship leaders is Matt

Redman of the Soul Survivor Church in Watford, England. Matt tells the story in his recent book, *The Unquenchable Worshipper,* about how his pastor challenged their people to push beyond the trappings of great musicians and exciting music to rediscover the heart of worship.

Matt explains that several years ago, the passion that had always characterized their corporate worship services at Soul Survivor was noticeably lacking. The music was good, the team was talented, but the people had started to rely on those things and to see *them* as the offering of worship. The "stuff"—who was playing that day, what songs were chosen, how good the system sounded—was dictating their experience.

Mike, the pastor, decided to do something drastic. For a season, he would strip it all away, the musicians, the instruments, everything down to the worshipers themselves. They would learn to worship from within, to give themselves to God, instead of just singing along. He would ask the people every time they entered the sanctuary, "What are you bringing as your offering?"

After a time, the church discovered a deeper, more profound place of worship than it had known before. The trappings eventually reappeared, but Matt says, "The songs of our hearts had caught up with the songs of our lips." I found it especially interesting that out of that experience, Matt wrote the very popular praise song, "The Heart of Worship":

When the music fades,
And all is stripped away,
And I simply come;

Longing just to bring something that's of worth

That will bless Your heart.

I'll bring You more than a song,

For a song in itself

Is not what You have required.

You search much deeper within

Through the way things appear:

You're looking into my heart.

I'm coming back to the heart of worship,

And it's all about You,

It's all about You, Jesus.

I'm sorry, Lord, for the thing I've made it,

When it's all about You,

It's all about You, Jesus.[7]

Presence based worship leaders are worshipers first and musicians second. They are quite familiar with the Presence themselves because they have worn a path to the feet of Jesus. They know that to lead people into a genuine encounter with the Presence of God, they must simply worship and get so caught up in it that others follow. Real worship is not something you can manipulate, however it is something that Presence based worship leaders recognize. Veteran worship leader Brian Doerksen agrees:

> When I stand before people to lead worship, I know full well that I am not able to convince anyone to worship God by trying to talk them into it or by stirring their emotions. My first desire and task is to worship God myself, to give him my life and love again....[8]

That is the mark of a Presence based worship leader—she ministers to God regardless of who else is doing what. It's not about great production or even audience participation. It's about giving ourselves as an offering and ascribing honor and glory to the Lord. Ron Kenoly, another well-known worship leader of the Jubilee Christian Center in San Jose, California explains how he knows when genuine worship has been achieved:

> I'm often asked how I know when I have accomplished my job. The truth is that it's not something I see with the natural eye. I do not have a written formula. Sometimes I know I'm finished when I can feel the presence of the Lord in the room so strong that I know the only thing left for me to do is to get out of God's way. Many times it is not appropriate for me to say or do anything.[9]

Worshiping God in the Presence based church is not just another activity on the agenda for Sunday morning. It is the first and most important reason for existence. The church emulates the Levitical worship that took place in the tabernacle of Moses. The people know to wait on God, they extol his greatness in personal and corporate worship, and they offer intercession in the context of worship. They are part of an emerging breed of worshipers that encapsulates the heart of Mary.

And that is just the point—it is the *heart* of the Presence based church that sets it apart, not the actions. Being Presence based is a character trait.

Martha and Mary, Scene II

Consider with me for a moment the second time Martha and Mary appear on stage in Scripture (John 11:1-44). This time their beloved brother Lazarus is sick. The narrator, the apostle John, sets the tone by telling us, "Jesus loved Martha and her sister and Lazarus." These were not just people in the crowd—they were dear friends of Jesus in a real and very human way. He cared deeply about them.

Knowing that Jesus was ministering in a neighboring town, Martha and Mary sent word to him to come right away so he could heal Lazarus. Jesus, however, had another plan, as he so often did, and instead of hurrying to the aid of his friends, he lingered for two more days in the town he was in. During that time, Lazarus died. By the time Jesus arrived in Bethany where the sisters lived, Lazarus had been in the tomb for four days. The mourning and grieving process was well under way.

It's about giving our-selves as an offering and ascribing honor and glory to the Lord.

As Jesus approached the house, Martha ran out to meet him and said, "Lord, if you had been here, my brother would not have died." It was a statement of Martha's faith, but at the same time, a haunting question for which she expected an answer—an explanation. What followed was a brief conversation between the two in which Jesus assured Martha that indeed Lazarus would live again, and tried to help her see with spiritual eyes what her mind simply couldn't understand.

After Martha returned to the house, Mary went to meet Jesus and she too said, "Lord, if you had been here, my brother would not have died." Mary however, as she uttered the words, fell into a heap at Jesus' feet and cried. For Mary, the exact same words had a completely different meaning. She wasn't *questioning* Jesus; she was *worshiping* him. She wasn't looking for an explanation; she was looking for comfort from her Lord whom she trusted with childlike faith, even in unspeakable anguish.

Jesus' response is worth a thousand words. "When Jesus saw her weeping…, he was deeply moved in spirit and troubled." He didn't try to explain anything to Mary. He simply cried with her, and together they went to the tomb. This was the only time during his entire ministry that we are told that Jesus actually wept. Of course, it had been in Jesus' heart all along to raise Lazarus from the dead to bring glory to the Father, and that's exactly what he did.

Mary knows of no place that is more secure, more glorious, or more life affirming than the feet of Jesus. She sat at his feet in her living room filled with guests and wept at his feet during the wake for her brother. The Presence based church, like Mary, is always at the feet of Jesus—in good times and bad. It is where they bring their joy and their sorrow. Board meetings are at the feet of Jesus. Small groups worship at the feet of Jesus. The worship leaders usher the congregation to the feet of Jesus Sunday after Sunday after Sunday because there is no other place like it. Their first ministry is to him. Robert Stearnes writes about the heart of Mary:

> I believe the Holy Spirit is releasing to the church in this hour the heart of Mary—a simple belief that pure devotion to Him will bring true, lasting, personal change, which will then result in societal impact. This is our beginning place. This is the source of our activity. This is the place to which we seek to draw men and women—not to a system or institution or program—but to a real place at the feet of Jesus, near to His heart.[10]

The Worship Offering

Good worship is not attained simply through better technology or state of the art systems. There are consumer based churches in every city that have all the latest and most exciting technological capabilities and yet still have powerless, Presence starved worship because they don't understand the heart of Mary. George Barna asserts that some of today's most "effective" churches are learning this lesson:

> Simplicity in worship is more valuable than having a slick, over-produced event. Thus, at the very time when churches across the land are striving to achieve greater production values—full orchestras or bands, theatrical presentations, video projection systems, professional sound and lighting—the highly effective churches stand out for the ability to implement

such elements, but their determination is to forego many of the bells and whistles and instead go simple. Why? "This is worship. The more complex or riveting we make the process, the less people focus on God," was the simple explanation of one leader/ pastor.[11]

Sally Morgenthaler agrees that it is not the production, but the sincerity of worship that attracts people both to our churches and subsequently to Jesus:

> In our infatuation with the cosmetic, perhaps we have forgotten that what will both draw and keep people is worship that is not only culturally relevant, but real. Real worship is a lot more than this week's production. It is where we allow the supernatural God of Scripture to show up and to interact with people in the pews.[12]

Jack Hayford describes the transformation that he initiated in his own church as he began to understand Presence based worship:

> More than tightly regimented gatherings, concerned over the aesthetics, mechanics and academics of our time together, we began to prioritize providing an unpressured portion of the service for freely flowing songs of praise and adoration—often songs directly expressive of the Scriptures.
>
> Such worship will cause us to be awed by His presence and fall in love with His person.[13]

All of these teachers are saying the same thing—true worship is not defined by the vehicle, nor is it confined by style, knowledge, ability or history. It is a heart issue.

Moreover, true worship can happen at any time in any place. No single type of church has a corner on the worship market, and we must take care not to get sucked into this kind of stereotyping. Remember that the original Levites worshiped in a variety of ways and positions. Sometimes they were quiet, other times they were quite exuberant. At times they bowed or lay prostrate before the Lord, while at other times they danced.

Randy Harvey, worship leader and senior pastor of The Crossing Church north of Houston, recalls being invited as part of a band to do a concert for a Catholic youth gathering. Having done several similar events prior to that, the band thought they had an idea of what to expect—namely apprehension, especially to worship.

They started the concert with a couple of high energy songs and then moved into upbeat worship. To their surprise and delight, the kids seemed to know the songs and began praising God. The band felt a collective sense of relief and excitement. Randy relates what happened next:

> That's when the two swinging doors at the back of
> the auditorium flew open. There was a priest with
> the black outfit on, the white collar, the long silver
> crucifix, maybe 40ish. He was holding a big, vintage
> gold cross (big as in 18 inches high and 16 inches
> across!). He was the most "Catholic" looking thing

you could imagine, and seemed very out of place with the mood in the room and the praise that we were enjoying. For a few seconds I thought it was all over.

That's when the unexpected happened. He lifted the cross about shoulder high and began to "juke" it back forth, dancing down the center isle, looking upward in praise to God and smiling ear to ear. He actually ignited an even greater sense of worship in the room! He found a place to stand near the front and lifted the cross as high as he could, still dancing with it, and he praised with excitement in affirmation to the presence of the Holy Spirit.

I was awestruck. I couldn't stop crying. I left that night and thanked God all the way home for letting me see religious paradigms falling—for forgiving my arrogance and pride.[14]

Worship has the ability to transcend any barrier—language, education, age, tradition, or culture—to bring people into oneness in the Presence. It has a unifying effect. In many communities this is apparent in city-wide gatherings in which the body of Christ comes together just to worship. No preaching, no denominational sales pitches or promotions, no hidden agendas, just worship. Joseph Garlington observes that "the shock wave of our praise is unaffected by distance, different time zones, or different languages, cultures, and political systems. It is a spiritual force to be reckoned with...."[15]

While working on this book, I heard this worship song for the first time, even though it was written several years ago. It seemed to encapsulate in a simple chorus the book's silhouette. Indeed, the Presence based church longs to worship at the feet of the Lord, knowing that just one glance into the face of the Savior will bring more change than a lifetime of sermons or church activities. The heart of Presence based worship, regardless of the style or outward expression, is simply this: Will you come and meet with us?

> I will run to the cleft of the mountain and wait for you
> Will you come and meet with me?
> I will wait at the cleft of the mountain for you to pass by
> Will you come and meet with me?
> Oh, what a joy it would be
> Just for a moment to lay at the feet of the Lord
> More than anything, that's what I long for
> And oh, what a change it would bring
> Just to look deep in the face of the King who gave all
> You gave everything so you could meet with me
> Will you meet with me?[16]

The Presence based church worships to welcome the living God. Their adoration is an invitation for him to come and dwell in the midst of his people and make himself known. Words like desperation, hunger, need, yearning and desire all go into worship visioning and practice. The mystery and greatness of God drives their holy dissatisfaction to know him better—he is never taken for granted! They want nothing more than to meet with him, and so they wait…and worship…and wait…and worship.

Discussion Questions

1. Why is unity in the body of Christ so important?

2. Worship can be very unifying. Can it also be divisive? What makes it one or the other?

3. The author asserts that true worship has little to do with style or production. Do you agree? Why?

4. What characterized worship around the Ark under Moses, David and Solomon? Could this progression be a pattern for personal and/or corporate worship? Discuss.

5. What do you think Martha was feeling when she said to Jesus, "Lord, if you had been here, my brother would not have died"? What do you think Mary was feeling when she said the same words? Why did Jesus respond so differently?

6. What does it mean to be "at the feet of Jesus"?

7. Why is being Presence based not just a Sunday morning issue?

THE NEW ORDER OF LEVITES

Recall that the Levites were the tribe of Israelites designated to care for the tabernacle and watch over the Ark day and night. Alfred Edersheim describes the night watches around the tabernacle:

> At night guards were placed in twenty-four stations about the gates and courts. Of these twenty-one were occupied by Levites alone; the other innermost three jointly by priests and Levites. Each guard consisted of ten men; so that in all two hundred and forty Levites and thirty priests were on duty every night.[1]

In addition to worshiping and ministering to the Presence of the Lord as a full time job, they cared for the details of moving and maintaining the Holy Place. They were not required to contribute in any other way to community life—their food and other provisions were supplied through offerings from the other eleven tribes. The Levites were set apart.

The Levites gazed upon the tabernacle around the clock because God lived there. In shifts they would come and minister to the Lord. No need for bulletins because the program was worship, worship and more worship. It never ceased. As they worshiped, they waited on God in awe with anticipation and expectation. They didn't hang a clock on the wall or take notice of time because time was absorbed by his beauty. It only had meaning when they were away from the Presence. He was all consuming, exceedingly worthy of their focus and service, and the Levites gladly spent themselves on their inheritance. While other tribes made site plans for their land, the Levites set their sights on him with joy because he was Jehovah, the God of Israel!

The new breed of worshiper with the "Mary" heart is not really new at all. The worshipers that are emerging now in Presence based churches are simply a new generation of Levites, called by the Holy Spirit to minister to the Presence of God as a lifestyle, not just from 11-12 on Sunday mornings. God is raising them up all over the country.

George Barna describes the spirit of Levitical worship:

Effective churches teach their people that you can never give God too much worship; He revels in it. Worship is not meant to be simply a Sunday morning activity—it is not something you turn on at 11:00 a.m. on Sunday and switch off at noon, not to be worried about for the next 167 hours. Worship is meant to be a regular part of our daily existence.[2]

Church consultants today say that between 20 and 25 minutes of worship during a Sunday morning service is the "right" amount. However, for this new Order of Levites, 20 minutes a week amounts to little more than spiritual starvation. For them, like their Old Testament counterparts, worship is life, and to live is to worship. The truth is, we should all be preparing ourselves for continual praise and adoration of the Father because that's exactly what heaven will be like. Just read Revelation 4 and 5. John Piper, in his book, *Let the Nations Be Glad*, agrees:

> Missions is not the ultimate goal of the church. Worship is. Missions exists because worship doesn't. Worship is ultimate, not missions, because God is ultimate, not man. When this age is over, and the countless millions of redeemed fall on their faces before the throne of God, missions will be no more. It is a temporary necessity. But worship abides forever.[3]

Around the throne of God, we will not be able to contain our worship to once a week or even once every day because his full glory will be so awesome and resplendent that as soon as we see it, we will cease to care about anything else. We will spend eternity pouring forth praise and adoration to Jehovah and will never grow weary or bored! The worship of heaven will be far beyond what our minds can even conceive, so we might as well start training now.

Robert Stearnes foretold of a "company of End-Time Levites" in his book, *Prepare the Way*:

> We will enter into hours and days of extended waiting in His presence. We will hear His heartbeat and know His voice. We will be overcome with one relentless, insatiable craving—more of Him. Past the outer courts of our own need, worship will be all about ministering to the Lord Himself. A holy company of End-Time Levites will be brought forth in the nations of the earth to tend to the flame of the Lord, seeing that it does not burn out day or night. Jealousy for His house will consume us, and once again His house will be called a house of prayer for all nations. Religious machinations will cease as we are undone by his glory and His love. An hour in His presence, gazing into his eyes of beauty, will accomplish more than weeks of counseling and human effort at healing our souls. We will understand that the Healer *is* healing, and simply being with Him cleanses, refreshes and satisfies.[4]

An insatiable craving for more of God—yes, that is the Presence based church. Not satisfied with an occasional taste of the Presence, but wanting a steady diet of it every day. This new generation of Levites never takes the Presence for granted. With hearts turned Godward and a passion to worship him and minister to him above and beyond anything else, they are fulfilling God's call for believers to be his "chosen people, a royal priesthood, a holy nation, a people belonging to God, that [we] may declare the praises of him who called [us] out of darkness into his wonderful light" (1 Peter 2:9).

Oh how we need this kind of worship in the church! I was recently in South Dakota conducting a Prayer Encounter weekend, and on Sunday morning around noon I was jogging in the downtown YMCA. Out the window I could see several downtown churches and noticed that by 12:15 they were all quiet. Services were over, the parking lots were vacant and the people were gone.

How tragic that we have accepted the traditional Sunday morning corporate gathering as adequate worship for the King of kings!

It struck me as I looked over the large cathedrals, with their spiraling steeples and well-preserved stained glass windows, how many days and hours of their existence those buildings had stood empty, just as they were now. It would be a week before people would once again come and fill the sanctuaries with any kind of worship or prayer. How tragic that we have accepted the traditional Sunday morning corporate gathering as adequate worship for the King of kings! One of the enemy's greatest lies is convincing Christians that just being in the building for a service constitutes "worship."

A Lifestyle of Worship

The new Levites don't wait for church to worship. Worship fills their personal lives. They are private worshipers in their homes, in their cars, during their lunch breaks, and with their children. Any place can become their temple in which to bow, wait, sing, dance or shout to the Lord.

The Holy Spirit is their worship leader, and it is by his prompting that they continually minister to the Presence. Jesus said, "Yet a time is coming and has now come when the true worshipers will worship the Father in spirit and truth, for they are the kind of worshipers the Father seeks. God is spirit and his worshipers must worship in spirit and in truth" (John 4:23-24). The Holy Spirit inspires praise and can open mouths and hearts to bring forth expressions of love for God. He can breathe life into liturgy and stimulate creativity. He pulls back the natural veil to reveal the splendor and wonder of Jesus, the new Ark.

David was a private worshiper throughout all the phases of his life as a shepherd, a fugitive, and then a king. And because he worshiped personally, the Presence spilled out from his spirit and overflowed into his public life. David, like Moses, had a habitual hunger for God. He was not a God taster or a God tourist, he was, as Tommy Tenney called it, a God chaser.[5] The desire with which he consistently sought after God created a vacuum in his heart to be filled by the Presence, and God felt welcomed and invited. David was Presence filled and Presence based and as a result, God had a strong hand on his life.

Worship in the early church was of a personal nature as well. Mostly it took place in homes and jails, since formal services in designated church buildings would not come along for another 300 years after the resurrection. Their worship was spontaneous, personal and serendipitous. Good corporate worship must begin in the individual hearts of the worshipers.

As the people of the Presence based church cultivate their private praise lives, they become like a myriad of tributaries, converging on Sunday morning into a great river of worship to "make glad the city of God" (Psalm 46:4). It is their personal worship during the week that creates the atmosphere for God to move in their midst corporately. John Wimber, founder of the Vineyard movement, explains how he learned this principle:

> Now, during this time when we were stumbling around corporately in worship, many of us were also worshiping at home alone. During these solitary times we were not necessarily singing, but we were bowing down, kneeling, lifting hands, and praying spontaneously in the Spirit.... We noticed that as our individual worship life deepened, when we came together there was a greater hunger toward God. So we learned that what happens when we are alone with the Lord determines how intimate and deep the worship will be when we come together.
>
> About that time we realized our worship blessed God, that it was for God alone and not just a vehicle of preparation for the pastor's sermon. This was an

exciting revelation. After learning about the central place of worship in our meetings, there were many instances in which all we did was worship God for an hour or two.[6]

It is this truth that stirs the worship leader in the Presence based church to teach the people how to become private, daily worshipers of God. A worship team does not worship for the people; each person must worship from his own spirit. We are all created for God's pleasure, and he delights in our individual relationship with him. Therefore, in the Presence based church, the role of the worship leader during the services is not to entertain, but to facilitate the corporate expression of what is going on throughout the week. He knows that worship on Sunday morning is built in the prayer room, the living room and the individual hearts of the worshipers.

He knows that worship on Sunday morning is built in the prayer room, the living room and the individual hearts of the worshipers.

The Order of Levites being raised up is the new tribe of Presence keepers—guarding the sanctity and purity of worship in the church. One of the jobs of the Old Testament Levites was to make sure that procedures were followed when transporting the Ark of the Covenant and setting up the tabernacle. They adhered to the letter of God's instruction when the Ark had to be moved, for example, always using the poles to carry it, and not an ox cart, as David had mistakenly done. Similarly, the Levites today guard against "new carts" in the church. They understand and respect the Presence and they know how to attend to him when he shows up. Always anticipating his arrival, they help establish and protect Presence protocol. Their trademark is humility; their worship style simple and biblical.

The original Levites were also given the job of maintaining the fire on the altars, which could only come from the Mercy Seat and was to burn continually. Because this fire came only from the Presence, it was different than pagan fires that burned on pagan altars. Its origination was holy and distinctive. Aaron's two sons died because they brought fire into the temple from the outside. The new Levites are aware of the dangers of "unauthorized fire." They are skeptical of fads and human agendas in worship that don't originate from the Holy Spirit. Praise performances and rituals that glorify people or rely on gimmicks to stir emotions find no audience with the Levites. Anything less than pure, God-centered worship is unacceptable.

The Levites also tend to their pastors much as their biblical counterparts assisted the priests. With special, fragrant oil they made according to God's careful instructions, the ancient Levites anointed the priests before they entered the Holy of Holies. The oil was sacred, and was to be used only to consecrate the priests and the tabernacle articles. In addition to anointing the priests, the Levites also washed and dressed them to prepare them for ministry. The new Order of Levites anoints their pastors with prayer, washes them with the Word, and dresses them in the full armor of God for protection. They delight in keeping their shepherds safe from the bites of angry sheep. With devotion, they claim favor and power for their pastor, and because they honor their leaders, God will honor them.

Finally, the Old Testament Levites made special incense to burn on the altar in the tabernacle as a pleasing fragrance to the Lord. Like the oil, it was considered holy and was not to be made or used for any other purpose. The incense we offer to God is praise, and the new Presence keepers love to bring this offering to the altar. Rich, biblical worship rises from their hearts and their lips like a pleasing fragrance for his pleasure.

Wardrobe of Praise

For decades, the "garment of praise" worn by many of our mainline denominations in America has been a straightjacket. The act of worship was tied down and tethered to rituals, which may have been meaningful at one time, but over the years became empty, repetitive patterns. As a result, in too many churches, praise became empty and repetitive also. The biblical concept of praise was lost on generations of churchgoers that were scripturally undernourished, particularly from the Old Testament, and had become totally disconnected from the earliest practices of their own denominations. I know for a fact that many United Methodists today would be shocked to read the journals of John Wesley, and would adamantly deny having any ties to the fanatical worship that characterized his meetings.

The Bible, however, tells a different story of praise. Seven different Hebrew words make up the complete palette of "praise" throughout the Old Testament:

1. YADAH means *to worship with extended hand.* It signifies total dependence on God. David exclaims, "I will praise you as long as I live, and in your name I will lift up my hands" (Psalm 63:4). Interestingly, the opposite of YADAH would be *the wringing of the hands.*

2. TOWDAH comes from the same root as Yadah, but has a slightly different meaning. It means *extension of the hand in adoration or acceptance.* It is used to thank God for things received as well as things not yet received. Therefore it has the underpinnings of faith.

3. HALAL (the word from which we get hallelujah) means *to be clear, to shine, to boast, to show, to rave or celebrate, to be clamorously foolish.*

4. SHABACH means *to address in a loud tone, to command, triumph, glory, to shout.* David wrote, "Clap your hands, all you nations; shout to God with cries of joy" (Psalm 47:1).

5. BARAK means *to kneel or bow, to bless God as an act of adoration.* The negative could mean to curse God or commit blasphemy. "Come, let us bow down in worship, let us kneel before the LORD our Maker..." (Psalm 95:6).

6. ZAMAR means *to touch the strings.* It is used to describe worship with instruments, mostly rejoicing.

7. TEHILLAH means *to sing, to laud.* "Sing joyfully to the LORD, you righteous; it is fitting for the upright to praise him. Praise the LORD with the harp; make music to him on the ten-stringed lyre. Sing to him a new song" (Psalm 33:1-3).[7]

The new Order of Levites are finding, even within the context of their own denominational parameters, times and ways to express their devotion to God utilizing all the forms of praise. They are not merely offering a song; they are offering *themselves* as the sacrifice in total humility and without regard for reputation. They are sold out and unashamed. Matt Redman wrote how he feels about creativity in worship:

> As worshippers of Jesus today, we also need to cultivate this sort of unpredictability in our worship. When we come before the living God, there should always be aspects of the fresh and the surprising. These things are a sign of life. Worship is meant to be an encounter, an exciting meeting place where love is given and received in an unscripted manner.[8]

When I visited Korea, one of the things that impressed me so much about the people in general, and the Christians in particular, was their level of humility. The power of the prayer movement in that country is easily understood when you witness the way they so willingly posture themselves before God in total humility and vulnerability. They are not ashamed to bow or lie prostrate to pray or wait on the Lord. They are not afraid to cry out to him or lift their voices in worship and adoration. Their total submission to and dependence on God is expressed through their physical body.

The Presence based worshiper knows the same secret that the Korean Christians know—that there is an undeniable link between our physical position and our attitude. Posture affects how we relate to God. Notice that I said it *affects* how we relate; it doesn't *determine* how we relate. One can be totally submitted in spirit while standing just as one can be kneeling or bowing while still harboring pride in his heart. Nevertheless, something about the bodily expression of being on your knees or lying on your face makes it easier for you to submit yourself completely in mind and spirit to worship or prayer.

> *Something in us longs to fall into submission to our Creator and relinquish control...*

When Mary encountered Jesus, she postured herself as a servant, at his feet. When the Levites encountered the Presence of God in the tabernacle, they fell to the floor. Something in us longs to fall into submission to our Creator and relinquish control, and when we sense him near, that is exactly what happens.

Unfortunately for us, we live in a society that tends to value power over submissiveness, resourcefulness over dependence, and confidence over humility. This is especially true for men in our society. The latter are all seen as signs of weakness, a notion that drives us to stand tall, keep it together, and never let our guard down. Our all-American philosophy of life comes straight from the John Wayne school of success: "Never let 'em see you sweat!" In other words, never let on that you need something, and never reveal vulnerability.

Yet isn't that what we must do in order to truly worship? "Come, let us bow down, in worship, let us kneel before the LORD our Maker" (Psalm 95:6). The new Order of Levites loves to bow or kneel before God in worship as a physical expression of surrender. They know that something powerful happens when our mind, spirit and body all come into alignment. When we assign the flesh to mortality, the Spirit in us is enlivened. At that point, we are no longer offering worship to God with just our lips; we have *become* the offering, broken and dependent on his merciful acceptance.

William Temple once wrote of what it means to surrender in worship:

> Worship is the submission of all our nature to God. It is the quickening of conscience by his holiness; the nourishment of mind with his truth; the purifying of imagination by his beauty; the opening of the heart to his love; the surrender of will to his purpose—and all this gathered up in adoration, the most selfless emotion of which our nature is capable and therefore the chief remedy for that self-centeredness which is our original sin and the source of all actual sin.[9]

Perhaps the humility of the Levites had something to do

with their spiritual ancestry. A look at their family heritage reveals another interesting glimpse into the redemptive heart of God. The 12 tribes of Israel descended from the 12 sons of Jacob. In Genesis 49, Jacob speaks a prophetic blessing over each of these sons, meant not only for them but also for the tribes that they would sire. However, listen to what Jacob had to say about Levi, from whom the Levites came:

> Simeon and Levi are brothers—their swords are weapons of violence. Let me not enter their council, let me not join their assembly, for they have killed men in their anger and hamstrung oxen as they pleased. Cursed be their anger, so fierce, and their fury, so cruel! I will scatter them in Jacob and disperse them in Israel (Genesis 49:5-7).

In light of the rest of the passage, Jacob didn't think very highly of these two boys, and certainly had nothing positive to say about them. They were apparently violent and cruel. Yet, when God chose the tribe to serve in the tabernacle with the priests, he specifically instructed Moses that the tribe of Levi would be his. Several times, the Lord stated emphatically, "They are to be mine." He explained to Moses that they were to serve the priests and the whole community by tending to the tabernacle and fulfilling the obligations of the Israelites before him. He had Moses set them apart and consecrate them to live and serve their lives in the temple.

I found it interesting that of all the tribes God could have chosen to be his attendants, he chose the descendants of Levi—

a man who was cursed by his own father and basically written off as no good. In other words, the original worship team came from "bad blood." It seems right in line with God's way of doing things to choose the unlikely, unimpressive and unqualified as his personal worshipers to be nearer to him than all the others. That he didn't choose the best or the finest for himself is just another testimony to God's uniqueness and grace toward us. I almost have to believe he was deliberately trying to send the message that worship has nothing to do with us—it's all about him. What we bring doesn't really matter. All he wants is all of us.

I have tried to imagine what it would have been like to be in the tabernacle in the wee hours of the morning when darkness still hovered over the camp and all was quiet. Stationed there to keep watch over the Ark, hundreds of Levites would have stood waiting, watching, gazing at the familiar yet still enchanting cloud between the cherubim. Some worshiped silently on their knees, some lay on the ground, while others stood guard. I don't imagine there was much conversation or movement in those pre-dawn hours, just the thick stillness of night pierced only by the reassuring glow of the Presence. How awesome it must have been!

So rewarding was their life as God's attendants that the Levites didn't mind that they received no land inheritance like the other tribes. Their inheritance was God himself (Deuteronomy 10:9). They were his and he was theirs. The pleasure of being in his Presence far outweighed any earthly riches.

The new Order of Levites gathers around the new Ark of the Covenant, Jesus, and meditates upon his majesty and splendor. Like Mary, they sit at his feet for hours listening and soaking up his Presence. He is their inheritance. They are impassioned to worship day and night, without regard to time or circumstance because the reward is great. His beauty and glory and mystery beckon all who taste it to come back for more.

This new generation of worshipers is bringing the church back to the heart of worship. The Presence based church worships because he is so worthy. It worships because he is mighty, jealous, lovely and merciful. It worships because one moment in the Presence of the Lord can relieve, repair, renew and rebuild. And because of Jesus, we no longer have to stay behind the veil. We can enter into the Holy Presence and be with him, just as Mary was with him.

Summary

From the last two chapters, we could begin to illustrate Mary's Presence based church like this:

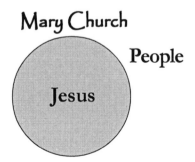

Mary Church

People

Jesus

<u>Presence Based Church</u>

1. Levitical Worship

Discussion Questions

1. Are we all called to be private worshipers? Are we all called to be among the New Order of Levites? Explain.

2. Describe a "lifestyle of worship."

3. Is your garment of praise a straightjacket? Why? Would you like a new wardrobe?

4. Discuss the John Piper quote on page 167.

5. What were some of the duties of the Old Testament Levites? How do the new Levites fulfill many of the same duties?

6. What does God desire from us as our worship offering?

7. How do you feel about bowing or lying on your face before the Lord? Live on the edge—take a moment right now and try it. If you are with a class, do it as a group and then discuss. If you are alone, jot down anything you hear or feel after you are done. You can worship in silence as the Levites did, or with music. But do not pray. Just be still before him and listen.

THE PRESENCE BASED CHURCH

I n talking about the worship life of the Presence based church, it would have been very easy for me to throw prayer into the same kettle because in reality I believe they function together and are, in fact, two sides of the same coin. I chose not to in this instance however, because it was important for me to convey the urgency I feel about how little we understand or engage in true worship. If there is only one thing that this book inspires in you, I hope it will be the desire to worship more. So many of our churches and denominations today are experiencing worship starvation, and the deficiency is crippling.

Over the past several months, as I have taught this message in various churches, it has become apparent to me that while some receive and understand what I'm saying, many only think they hear. But I can tell by their response that they really don't understand. They have fasted worship for so long that they have no idea what it's like to feast.

I was speaking in a church recently and before the session, I was talking with the worship leader and sharing some of these thoughts with him. I asked him, "What can you tell me that would help me teach people to worship more when they're not at church?" He looked puzzled. "I don't understand what you mean, Terry." He was a worship leader, yet the idea that people could worship outside the church service didn't register with him. His only frame of reference for worship was what happens on Sunday mornings.

Go to a consumer based church, and you'll hear people talk about worship: Which worship service do you go to? Present your tithe as an act of worship. What style of worship do you prefer? We're so glad you came to worship with us today.

But in the Presence based church, worship means something more. It's not just worship, but *worship*. It's an act that engages all that you are in loving all that he is. It's the force that brought Mary to the feet of Jesus, and the Levites to their knees before the Ark. Presence based worship is a response to a God who is so terrifyingly magnificent, yet so intimately known that praise and adoration burst forth naturally and without effort. It can not be contained. C.S. Lewis expressed it this way:

> I had never quite noticed that all enjoyment spontaneously overflows into praise... The world rings with praise—lovers praising their mistresses, readers their favourite poet, walkers praising the countryside, play-

ers praising their favourite game.... I had not noticed either that just as men spontaneously praise
whatever they value, so they spontaneously urge us
to join them in praising it: "Isn't she lovely? Wasn't it
glorious? Don't you think that magnificent?" The
psalmists in telling everyone to praise God are doing
what all men do when they speak of what they care
about.[1]

As the Mary church enjoys the sweet Presence of God,
their joy spontaneously erupts into praise and worship, which in
turn maintains an atmosphere that welcomes the Presence. This
mutual adoration of the people for God and God for his people
is what makes the Mary church feel distinctively different and
magnetic.

Prayer

As I said before, I could have lumped prayer together with
worship, because they are so closely related and prayer is the second most important hallmark of the Presence based church.
Prayer, like worship, invites the Presence of God to come. Jesus
said, "My house will be called a house of prayer..." (Matthew
21:13). A house is a dwelling place, built to be inhabited, not just
visited. I wrote at length in the book *Acts 29* about how the Holy
Spirit comes in answer to prayer, and how our prayers become
God's portal into the earth to work his will in lives, churches,
cities and regions.[2] His Presence inhabits the house of prayer.

Most Presence based churches have a prayer room, or at

least a designated place where prayer and worship can happen every day, if not 24-7. Because they want the Presence to be at the very center of all they do, the church leadership gives high visibility and priority to auxiliary prayer and worship places. They know that God desires and deserves to be ministered to regularly, not just on Sunday, and the prayer room can be the focus of that activity.

It is almost impossible to attend any [Presence based] church function in which prayer doesn't play a role.

Prayer rooms provide a central place for information management, where individual prayer requests, maps, missionary information, and various prayer lists can be organized. The subjects of different stations in the prayer room may include any or all of the following: global current events, developing countries and people groups, local government leaders, area schools, fire and police departments, gangs, answered prayers, the pastoral and staff families, the United States President and cabinet, other churches, children and youth. Presence based churches tend to have a healthy balance of local interest and worldwide awareness.

Most prayer rooms operate on a sign up basis, allowing individuals to reserve a regular weekly time slot. Some are designed for one person, while other larger rooms are divided up into separate spaces, allowing several people to be using the room at one time. In recent years, the harp and bowl centers designed to combine continuous worship with strategic prayer have popped up all over the country. These centers may be operated by one local church, or by several churches in a given area. They are an outgrowth of the Levite mentality, havens for the new Levites emerging in churches of all kinds for whom Sunday morning worship is simply not enough.

Organization is a key to the Presence based church prayer life because they take prayer seriously. They see it as one of the primary functions of the body, and so it is budgeted for and planned for with as much emphasis as any other ministry area. Prayer is integrated into every church activity—Sunday school, worship services, small groups, fellowship times, outreach, even board and committee meetings. It is almost impossible to attend any church function in which prayer doesn't play a role.

With so much emphasis on prayer, the Presence based church prayer coordinator is a trusted leader in the church. She understands that most of life happens during the week—at work, at school and at home—and wants to have someone available, as much as possible, to pray with people whenever needs arise. Some churches make their physical prayer rooms accessible to the public, while others advertise a phone number that people can call to receive prayer. In a church that is truly hungry for God's Presence, the prayer room is often the engine room that powers everything else.

The prayer life of the Presence based church is well-established, multifaceted and healthy. God doesn't impose himself where he's not invited, and in order to invite him, someone must be communicating with him. Though I've never been in a church where the pastor believed his people had no room to grow in prayer, it is a given that to be Presence based, a church's corporate prayer life must be past the trying stage and well on its way to maturity with several strong ministries in place and a solid percentage of involvement. The pastor actively encourages the individual prayer lives of his members as well.

However, just having a large number of working prayer ministries or a high percentage of people involved in them is not the only issue. Martha can sustain a few prayer ministries for activity's sake with one hand tied behind her back. Prayer in the Presence based church is not just another program. It is a means to an end, which ultimately is to invite the Presence of God. It is purposeful and passionate, operating generally on three different levels: caring for personal needs, praying for the lost to be saved, and seeking God for himself.

Prayer as a Ministry

The Mary church is full of compassion, much of which is demonstrated through a variety of personal prayer ministries. Jesus' love for people pours through the prayer time at the altar during every service, intercession that goes on in the prayer room, special prayer vigils, and crisis prayer teams. The Mary church knows that Jesus empathizes with the pain and struggles of this life, and that he stands willing and able to meet every need and comfort every hurting soul.

It is very important in the Presence based church that people have the opportunity to be ministered to personally through prayer. Individual prayer ministry is a priority at all levels and in every setting. Special ministry teams are trained to pray one-on-one with people, and the congregation as a whole gets a steady diet of prayer teaching and modeling. They are quick to pray for any situation—healing, finances, relationships, jobs, children, guidance, even lost dogs—and believe in faith for the answer. In the atmosphere of worship, many prayers are answered and the testimonies of God's goodness fuel even more prayer.

In addition to praying for people personally at every opportunity, the Presence based church usually has a significant prayer covering over each worship service. This may be accomplished in several ways. For example, people may come early to the sanctuary and pray, people may sign up to pray during a worship service in a separate room, a ministry team may take up positions among the congregation and pray throughout the service for those around them, or intercessors may pray in the days leading up to worship. Some churches have come up with their own creative ways to bathe worship services in prayer, and some use a combination of tactics.

At Countryside Christian Church in St. Petersburg, Florida, several hundred members come to pray for about one hour before each worship service. The prayer time actually melts right into praise and worship as the congregation arrives. At the Brooklyn Tabernacle in New York, 30-60 people pray in a prayer room for God to move in the service and for Jesus to be lifted up. In a Church of God in Lansing, Michigan, the balcony has been turned into a prayer room with one-sided glass overlooking the sanctuary. Each Sunday a prayer team observes the service from the balcony and prays as the Holy Spirit leads. It is unique because they can see what is going on and therefore pray very specifically, yet they are not confined to silence. They are able to pray out loud or together as a group without distracting the worshipers.

George Barna agrees that praying for the worship experience itself is a priority most effective churches share.[3] When the Holy Spirit comes in answer to prayer, everything goes better from the first song to the offering. Creativity in worship flows out of prayer, and the church discovers new and practical ways to express love for Jesus.

Prayer Evangelism

Second, beyond addressing personal needs, prayer in the Presence based church focuses on the kingdom agenda of bringing the lost into relationship with Jesus. There is a holy addiction among both the leadership and the congregation to regularly seeing people saved on Sunday and throughout the week. This realm of prayer aimed at pre-believers is called prayer evangelism, and has found hundreds of creative expressions over the past decade. Some of the largest prayer evangelism movements that have emerged include Prayer through the 10/40 Window (and other entire people groups), prayerwalking, Lighthouses of Prayer and city-wide spiritual mapping. In addition, these ideas spawned a library of books that not only explain the theology of prayer evangelism, but also document the astounding transformations that have taken place as a result of it.

Prayer evangelism incorporates several different kinds of prayer such as traditional intercession, compassion prayer and warfare prayer. Traditional intercessory prayer, for example, might mean simply praying over a list of names for salvation. One might pray for a loved one to have divine appointments with people who will talk with them about Jesus. Or one could pray for God to make himself real to a lost friend, and for the Holy Spirit to soften her heart to the gospel and convict her of her need for forgiveness and salvation.

Prayers of compassion—praying for the felt needs of pre-believers so that they might experience God's love for them and be saved—is another dimension of prayer evangelism. It is the extension of prayer as a ministry that targets unbelievers. Jesus always looked upon sinners with compassion and often met their physical needs in order to open the door to their hearts. He still demonstrates his love for his wandering children by touching them where they hurt the most. As his Presence enwraps them, the taste of his grace is too sweet to turn down.

By praying for the felt needs of pre-believers in the context of our daily lives, we release the Presence to move and work in coffee houses, office buildings, subways, homes, grocery stores and banks. The Presence based church creates opportunities to take the Presence out into the community by reaching out through prayer.

For example, many churches are using simple prayer boxes placed in businesses to reach out to the marketplace with compassion. We call this ministry *Box 3:16* and offer a set of materials that churches can use to get started. It is a creative way to intercept the pain of unchurched people and offer them prayer and hope in Christ Jesus. Other churches establish lighthouses of prayer in crime ridden neighborhoods to invite the Presence to turn the tide. Some of these have been so successful that apartment landlords have actually given other units to the churches or ministries willing to set up a lighthouse in an attempt to salvage areas that seem hopelessly lost to illegal or destructive activity. Another creative prayer outreach is a ministry called Master Media based in Los Angeles. They came up with the idea of praying for media and entertainment celebrities to be radically changed by Jesus Christ so that many might be affected by their witness.

Just as Presence based churches are creative in worship, they are innovative in prayer evangelism, finding new ways to address the unique needs of their community through prayer. At the leading of the pastor, they are driven by the compassion of Jesus for the wounded, the lonely and the discounted.

Sometimes, in praying for the lost, it is necessary to take authority over evil and break through barriers in order to set someone free to hear the gospel. Ultimately, salvation is the work of the Holy Spirit, and for every soul a spiritual battle must be won in the heavenly realm. This is the role of warfare prayer.

The Bible says that the enemy veils the minds of unbelievers to the message of salvation. It is his top priority to confuse their thoughts and close their ears so that they can not hear or understand how much Jesus loves them. When the enemy has this kind of a foothold in a person's life, only the Holy Spirit can set him free. As we pray, the Presence begins to pull back the veil, making known the truth. We pray to evict evil and claim territory for the kingdom, be it an individual life or a definable area such as a school, a neighborhood, or a county. Just as Dagon crumbled in the Presence of the Ark, so the powers and principalities of this world crumble in the Presence of Jesus. Balanced, biblical spiritual warfare, when combined with traditional forms of intercession and motivated by compassion, can change the spiritual climate of an area.

Ultimately, salvation is the work of the Holy Spirit, and for every soul a spiritual battle must be won in the heavenly realm.

Steve Hawthorne and Graham Kendrick write about our position before the throne in spiritual warfare:

> Get right to the core of the war. Before you come against anything or anyone, come reverently to the Most High. Come before God in his throne room. His courts are in session. His throne presides over all spiritual war. If angelic forces are to be sent to engage in battle, they will take their assignments from God's throne. The dreadful and beautiful King of

creation has named you to be his child. You have bold, confident access through faith in Jesus. Come near and make your appeal.[4]

The Presence based church will use all the tools in the arsenal to expose their little corner of the world to the Presence of God because they know that one glimpse of Jesus can do more than a lifetime of human effort. They are God-dependent, and prayer is their lifeline for help, hope and healing.

Outside the Camp – First Love Prayer

The most distinguishing aspect of the Presence based church's prayer life that sets it apart from others is not actually any of the utilitarian ministries I've just described. Those are all important for sure, and definitely make up one part of the Presence based church's personality. But they have one thing in common—they all seek the *hand* of God. In other words, every facet of prayer I have talked about to this point is motivated by a need.

There is a realm of prayer, however, that does not seek the hand of God. It seeks his face and his smile. It goes beyond praying for personal needs, and even beyond praying for the lost, into a world of prayer that few ever experience. It is the purist form of prayer that teeters so close to the edge of worship that it is difficult to tell where one stops and the other starts—that of praying to know God for no other reason except that he is worthy. It could be described as conversational worship, or worshipful prayer. It is the prayer of first love.

When two people are in love, particularly if it is first love, they need no reason to be together except the shear delight in the other's company. They spend long moments of silent exploration, gazing at one another as if every inch held a new revelation. They can talk for hours about anything or nothing because every conversation is a journey of intimate disclosure and discovery. They talk because they want to know more. They talk because they want to be known. They talk because their greatest joy is to see the other smile.

First love prayer is the prayer of healthy desperation, a yearning simply to know Jesus and be known by him, without crisis or expectation. It is motivated, not by need, but by infatuation, curiosity and passion. The benefit is not what one receives, but the joy of giving. E. Stanley Jones, who was a Methodist missionary, says this about prayer:

> The first thing [in prayer] is to get God. If you get him, everything else follows…allow God to get at you, to invade you, to take possession of you. He then pours his very prayers through you. They are his prayers—God-inspired, and hence, God answered.[5]

The Presence based church hungers to know God in the same way that Moses knew him on the mountain—to speak to him face to face as a man speaks with his friend. They long to discover his ways, his glory, his nature, his thoughts, his rest, his heart and his voice. With humility and endurance, they press against the veil of the spiritual realm until the image of God is visible.

Just as Moses went "outside the camp" to be with God in the Tent of Meeting (Exodus 33:7), the Presence based church goes beyond the familiar to seek God. They are always pushing past the successes of yesterday and going beyond the normal routine of church life to pray and experience God in new ways.

It is important to go outside the camp at times, because the lull of life's rhythm can numb us to the grandeur of God. The "camp" is what we are used to. It's the motion of church life—go to Sunday School, get coffee and a donut, visit in the foyer, go to church, sing songs, listen to the sermon, give an offering, shake the pastor's hand, take the kids home, put the Bible on the shelf until next Sunday, when we do it all again. We find a sort of comfort in the ritual. It's disconcerting when the pastor is gone and someone else is in the pulpit, or when the order of worship is different. Yet it is at the point that we deviate from the norm, even in the smallest way, that we often discover something that stirs us in a new and fresh way. God can reveal to us a new truth or a different aspect of his character that we have never seen before.

Jesus practiced the principle of going outside the camp in Luke 4. He withdrew to the wilderness in preparation for his public ministry. He broke away from the ordinary to spend 40 days with the Father. He also went outside the camp on numerous other occasions as in Mark 1:35-37, Luke 5:16, and Luke 6:12. In fact, the Garden of Gethsemane was a type of tent of meeting for him.

Paul also went outside the camp. After his conversion, he

went into the Arabian Desert for three years to consult with God. John, when placed on the isle of Patmos, used the time to seek God, and recorded his encounters in the book of Revelation.

Seeking God, romancing with him, deepens our spiritual understanding and faith. It greatly enhances God's ability to transform lives and impact communities through us. That is why we need to go outside the camp to seek God for all that he is. Vast knowledge and profound experience awaits the body of believers who can shake free from the familiar long enough to gaze at the heavens and keep fueling the fire of first love. [6] In the words of Oswald Chambers, "Rouse yourself up and look to God. Build your hope on Him. No matter if there are a hundred and one things that press, resolutely exclude them all and look to Him."[7]

Presence Evangelism

The Sally Morgenthaler book called *Worship Evangelism* which I have referred to several times gracefully yet boldly challenges some of the current worship trends and suggests that genuine worship invites "seekers" to draw closer to Jesus (seekers being the unchurched or unsaved). My copy is dog-eared and highlighted on every other page. To my knowledge, Sally's is the only book entirely devoted to worship evangelism and the only one, at least in recent years, to use the phrase.

Another friend and international prayer leader Ed Silvoso authored the book *Prayer Evangelism*,[8] which gives powerful testimony to the idea that strategic prayer can change the spiritual climate of an area, thereby changing everyone and everything in it. The basic premise—prayer invites the Presence of God and the Presence of God has an impact—has been written about in many other notable books throughout the past decade during what Peter Wagner referred to as a "prayer epidemic."

Together, the two concepts—worship evangelism and prayer evangelism—are the cornerstones for what I call *Presence Evangelism*, bringing people into the kingdom by exposing them to the Presence of God. Jesus established the basis for Presence evangelism when he said, "No one can come to me unless the Father who sent me draws him" (John 6:44). Only a personal experience with God himself can cause people to put their hope in the Son. When the Presence is real, the lost will either accept the gift of salvation or flee in conviction. There is no neutral ground in the Presence.

When the Presence is real, the lost will either accept the gift of salvation or flee in conviction.

I have always believed in the power of prayer to win the lost, and most of the books I have written would fall into the prayer evangelism category. But I have also always had a passion for worship, and been aware of the power of the Presence during worship to heal and save. Presence Evangelism has been the theology of my ministry for the past 25 years, and I've just now figured out what to call it!

David Garret, a father of the praise and worship movement from New Zealand, says about the power of worship to
bring people to Jesus:

> Not only is the Father looking through the Earth
> for worshipers (see John 4:23, 24), but worship it-
> self will become one of the greatest "tools" in bring-
> ing the nations of the earth to him.... As "worship
> in spirit and truth" is given back to the Creator from
> every tribe, and in every language, I believe this will
> be one of the greatest evangelistic tools ever seen.[9]

Our resources are so limited—we can't heal, save or set
free. Human presence may offer temporary comfort and conso-
lation, but it produces no dramatic life change. Only the Lord
God Almighty can do that. Life transformation or rebirth is solely
the work of the Creator himself. His Presence has been the change
agent from the beginning of time.

After a seminar in Mississippi, a lady came up to me and
told me how she had become convinced of the power of the
Presence to bring a person to salvation. She explained that her
husband, who was a state senator at the time, was unsaved despite years of praying in his behalf. She put his name on several
prayer lists and began praying that he would sense the Presence
of God. He told her later that he started to have the strangest
feelings while at work that God was watching him, and the divine
surveillance made him uncomfortable. He tried to shake it, but it
wouldn't go away. Eventually, it was that discernible Presence of
God encircling and nudging him that brought him to the point

of repentance and salvation. God's manifest Presence alone is powerful and inescapable.

In Steve Macchia's book *Becoming a Healthy Church*, he tells the story of a pizza delivery person walking into the new ministry center of Community Covenant Church in Rehoboth, Massachusetts. Ten feet into the building, he stopped and asked, "What's going on here? What's this presence?"[10]

Where his Presence is being manifested, God's glory is evident. When the Presence fell on the Mercy Seat of the Ark, his glory filled the tabernacle to such an extent that no one could go near. His Presence was *noticeable*.

Think about it. If God were to manifest his Presence in your church, shouldn't it be just as noticeable as it was in the tabernacle? Is God not that same God that descended in the Holy Place and rested among his chosen people in fire and cloud? Is he not the same God who, from the Mercy Seat, displayed his power and authority, guided and governed the Israelites, gave them victory over their enemies, demonstrated his favor and love, established his uniqueness and offered atonement for sin?

Where God's Presence is being manifested today, the same results are evident. Humility and uncommon zeal characterize people of the Presence because they have seen his power and know of his authority in the earth. Where the Presence is, wisdom and peace prevail through his guidance. Pathways become clear and sound decisions are made. In the Presence, people gain victory over habits or emotions that have held them captive for years. Relationships are healed, lives are transformed, joy is evident and the powers of darkness are forced to retreat. In the Presence, many call on the name of Jesus and are saved in response to the wave of supernatural love and grace that penetrates their spirits. If these things are not happening in our churches with regularity, then we must ask ourselves by what evidence do we claim to know and offer the Presence of God?

If God were to manifest his Presence in your church, shouldn't it be just as noticeable as it was in the tabernacle?

One of the subjects I brought up earlier in the context of the consumer based church was marketing. It is a hot button among pastors and church leaders that can generate strongly differing opinions. Some highly esteemed writers and teachers feel marketing the church compromises the integrity and purity of the gospel. Others believe that marketing is absolutely essential to the church's success today. But the question I have to ask is this: As churches, why do we need to market, i.e., spread the word that we exist? If the Presence of God were even one tenth as real in our churches today as it was in the tabernacle of Israel, the whole world would know about it. The issue to me is not so much whether marketing is good or bad, but why, given the indescribable, beyond imagination awesomeness of the God we serve, it is necessary at all.

Presence evangelism focuses on the person of Jesus Christ,

inviting his Presence to dwell in our midst, because only by his Presence can the church make a difference to anyone or anything. The Presence based church works on an overflow principle—it seeks to enter into the Presence of God with such passion and consistency that the Presence ripple "overflows" onto unsuspecting bystanders. Like holy lava cascading down the sides of a volcano, the essence of God's holiness, power, love and grace runs here and there leaving kingdom results in its path.

David understood the principle of overflow, "My cup overflows" (Psalm 23:5b). The overflow of God's manifest Presence invited by worship and prayer produces real ministry. Tommy Tenney concurs:

> Everything good, including the things your local church does—from feeding the poor, to rescuing babies at the pregnancy counseling center, to teaching kids in the Sunday school classes—should flow from the presence of God. Our primary motivating factor should be, "We do it because of Him and because it is His heart."[11]

The ministry model of the New Testament was Presence evangelism all the way. The disciples went from town to town, praying, worshiping and ministering in the power of the Presence, and people were saved. They didn't teach seminars, organize social gatherings, or argue points of theology with their critics. Jim Cymbala asserts:

> The apostles weren't trying to finesse people. Their communication was not supposed to be "cool" or

soothing. They aimed for a piercing of the heart, for conviction of sin. They had not the faintest intention of asking, "What do people want to hear? How can we draw more people to church on Sunday?" That was the last thing in their minds. Such an approach would have been foreign to the whole New Testament.[12]

Instead they simply ministered in the very real and powerful Presence of their Lord and the results spoke volumes. They lifted up Jesus and people were healed. They focused on him alone, and became the most sought after, controversial, effective evangelists that ever lived.

The Presence in the early church produced dramatic results. In Acts 3, a lame man was healed and thousands of people believed in Jesus as a result. Later in the home of Cornelius, Peter began talking about the Lord Jesus and the Presence descended so powerfully that Cornelius' entire family was saved. Paul had such an encounter with the Presence on the road to Damascus that he was immediately converted and transformed from a Christian hating thug into a gospel gorilla. In fact, Paul's experience was so profound, that he never lost his hunger for more of God. Even after years of ministry—sharing Christ, planting churches, being raised from the dead and persecuted for his mission—Paul, a true leader among leaders of the faith, said, "I want to know Christ and the power of his resurrection and the fellowship of sharing in his sufferings…" (Philippians 3:10). The book of Acts is full of examples of Presence wrought, Presence centered, Presence drawn evangelism that swept like wildfire across cities and regions.

If churches today yearned half as much for the Presence of God as they do for the badges of cultural acceptance, we would scarcely be able to accommodate the influx of pre-believers that would come rushing through our doors for a deep drink of something spiritually real. People are thirsty for the living water, a personal encounter with a living God, and no degree of human involvement or techno-gospel production can satisfy their souls. The consumer based church is a mirage that promises refreshment, but delivers an empty cup. Only the Presence of God can quench their thirst and fill them.

The Revelation of Jesus

People ask me all the time, "How do you sustain continual prayer and worship in a congregation?" My answer is the revelation of Jesus. What the Holy Spirit reveals to us about the Son gives us passion and energy to pursue even more. How can we spend an hour in the prayer room? Discover the profound wisdom revealed in Jesus. How can we worship at home and in our cars? Behold his captivating beauty. At the unveiling, people will fall, smitten in their hearts by his astounding glory and exhilarated by his nearness. The revelation of Jesus is the inspiration and reward for those who diligently seek him.

I will say again that the revelation of Jesus can not be attained or earned; it is given sovereignly by God. He reveals the Son to us little by little as we wait on him with anticipation. Like an artist cherishes his greatest work, God longs to reveal Jesus to us, but will only entrust the mystery to those who will take time to appreciate its exquisite perfection.

Jesus told Peter that upon the rock of revelation, he would build the church, and the gates of hell would not prevail against it (Matthew 16:18). If our churches are not prevailing against the wickedness of the world—and perusing the headlines on any given day would give one the impression that they are not—perhaps it is because we have lost sight of Jesus.

Robert Stearnes says the enemy "has sought to defeat us by diluting our passion for Jesus and diverting us from our divine purpose."[13] When we place people on center stage as the focus of ministry, relegating Jesus to the role of mascot in the church, we forfeit the power that God made available in his name through the covenant. If he does not go before us into battle and command our complete trust and loyalty, we will not be the victorious, prevailing church we are intended to be.

People are thirsty for the living water, a personal encounter with a living God, and no degree of human involvement or techno-gospel production can satisfy their souls.

Paul understood the revelation of Jesus and knew that it was only by this revelation that he could preach the gospel:

Now to him who is able to establish you by my gospel and the proclamation of Jesus Christ, according to the revelation of the mystery hidden for long ages past, but now revealed and made known through the prophetic writings by the command of the eternal God, so that all nations might believe and obey him—to the only wise God be glory forever through Jesus Christ! Amen (Romans 16:25-27).

But when God, who set me apart from birth and called me by his grace, was pleased to reveal his Son in me so that I might preach him among the Gentiles, I did not consult any man, nor did I go up to Jerusalem to see those who were apostles before I was... (Galatians 1:15-17).

Paul didn't receive the revelation in a crowded class room; he received it in a secluded desert, just as John received it on a penal island while in exile.

It is only by revelation through the Holy Spirit that people will understand the radical message of the gospel, and it is only by waiting, worshiping, and seeking at the feet of Jesus that we can hope to receive the revelation. Jesus is coming again, but the Presence based church lives off of his "coming" every hour and every day. Roberts Stearnes believes that as the new Order of Levites is raised up to worship, "the splendor and glory of Jesus Christ will capture the affections of the church in a new way. The body of Christ will rediscover Christ's personhood and majesty."[14]

I love the Old Testament feel of the transfiguration scene.

The cloud envelopes Jesus, Peter, James and John, and God speaks, "This is my Son, whom I love; with him I am well pleased. Listen to him!" (Matthew 17:5) Just as the Lord had descended on the mountain to give authority to Moses in front of the Israelites, he did the same for Jesus in front of the disciples. Upon seeing the indescribable glory of the new Ark of the Covenant, James and John fell face down, terrified. When they looked up, they saw "Jesus only" (Matthew 17:8 KJV).

"Jesus only" has always been and will always be the un-equaled crown jewel of heaven and earth for all of eternity. He stands at the pinnacle of all that the Presence based church is and does. It is all about him.

Summary

We could continue our illustration of the Presence based church by adding four more characteristics:

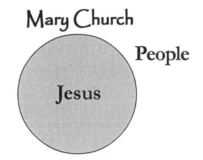

Presence Based Church

1. Levitical Worship

2. First Love Prayer

3. Compassion

4. Presence Evangelism

5. Revelation of Jesus

Discussion Questions

1. Why is prayer so vital to the Presence based church?

2. Would you describe the prayer relationship your church has with Jesus as "first date" (awkward, impersonal and informational) or "first love" (easy, intimate and pleasurable)?

3. Review the three levels of prayer in the Presence based church. Do you see all of these operating in your church? What about in your personal devotional life?

4. What does it mean to go "outside the camp"?

5. What is Presence evangelism?

6. Is the Presence of God discernible in your church? By what evidence?

7. Have you ever received a revelation of Jesus? Explain.

THE PRESENCE BASED PASTOR

The pressure on pastors today is enormous, especially in the consumer based church economy. They are expected to have the charisma and charm of Bing Crosby, the vision and ingenuity of Bill Gates, the leadership skills of Vince Lombardi, the tenacity and endurance of Lance Armstrong, the spiritual devotion of Billy Graham, and the family life of Ward Cleaver, all wrapped up in "guy-next-door" approachability. Consumer based pastors are like politicians whose careers depend on their ability to garner a large and loyal following.

The Presence based church, however, turns on different wheels. Its pastor, though he (or she) may have all of these qualities and employ them skillfully in leading the church, understands this truth—success by God's definition has nothing to do with what he brings to the table. It's not about him or his ability. It's about Jesus. He doesn't spend his time networking with influential people, hurrying from one church function to another, promoting his agenda, or trying to figure out how to razzle-dazzle the Sunday crowd because he knows that one thing and one thing only will make a difference—the Presence of God.

Humility

The one defining characteristic that I believe to be the common denominator among Presence based pastors is humility. They have a healthy desperation to know and understand the things of God, and a deep yearning for his abiding Presence in their lives and churches. Like Moses, they are intimate with God; yet never familiar enough to take for granted his blessing. With the excitement of a new believer they marvel easily at the ability of God and his working in daily lives. They are slow to judge and quick to believe because their faith is commensurate with his greatness.

Humility is not the absence of qualification; it is the absence of pride, pretension and arrogance. A humble person is modest in spirit and action, not seeking to draw attention or praise to himself. I mentioned earlier in the book that when Jesus walked the earth, he demonstrated the highest form of humility and dependence on God, even though he and God were one. It is this level of humility and dependence that the Presence based pastor strives to emulate.

The Presence based pastor hangs his personal weaknesses, and those of his church, on the front of the cross so that Jesus' power may be made perfect in them (2 Corinthians 12:9). He hangs his strengths on the back of the cross so that they are always obscured by its glory. Humility calls this pastor and his people to be servants in the body of Christ—generous, modest and supportive of other churches.

Humility is a fruit of the Spirit, and the Presence based church is so hungry for God that they are not interested in dominating the local church "ABC" battle—attendance, buildings and cash.[1] The more successful they become, the more humble and contrite they seem to be and the more they desire to pray. They refuse to play the numbers game and have no designs to manufacture a "self" kingdom. Ironically, I have noticed that churches that claim to be Presence based are usually not, because those that are have too much humility to say so!

Pastor Betterdish

The Presence based pastor wants to be a man of God, not of people. He spends time daily at Jesus' feet to know his ways, his heart and his glory. The revelation he receives is his greatest reward. Like Mary, he spends much of his "work" time waiting, worshiping, listening and seeking before the Lord. As a result, he is divinely imprinted and impassioned. His ministry is an overflow of the Presence in his life, not just an offering of his own gifts and resources. Let's nickname him "Pastor Betterdish" because he consistently chooses what Jesus himself deemed the "best portion."

Pastor Betterdish is a leader among the new Levites as a keeper of the flame, and the time he spends in the Presence keeps him refreshed and bold as the spiritual shepherd for his people. He is spiritually nourished by the Presence and it shows! While his consumer based counterparts struggle with feeling tired and used up, he feels energized about the call on his life. His enthusiasm is evident to his congregation, and they reap the benefits not only through his anointed preaching, but in the blessing he imparts to them each week. His messages are powerful and prophetic because he is in tune with God's heart and is hearing his voice every week.

With his eyes focused squarely on Jesus, Pastor Betterdish isn't easily distracted by superficial church squabbles or potential controlites who want to bend his ear. He is not readily swayed by emotions or opinions of men. He wants to fear God more than people.

His guide is the Presence. When it moves, he moves, and when it stays, he stays. He refuses to go anywhere or make any decision that isn't directed and confirmed by the Holy Spirit. Pastor Betterdish does not have to resort to politics and power plays to rally the people behind him. He wears the garment of authority placed on him by God and is ordained by the Presence in his own life.

Just as he guards his own time of personal devotion, Pastor Betterdish guards the Presence in the life of his church. His heart is very bent toward worship and he sees it as the most important component of the service, even more so than the sermon. He is committed to whatever will keep corporate worship fresh and real while nurturing the individual worship lives of his members. He works closely with the music minister and prayer coordinator to minimize distractions such as entertainment that glorifies people, and maximize acts of worship that invite the Presence. With finances, attention and time, he gives high priority to worship and prayer related activities because he knows they are the keys to creating a holy habitation. His desire is to minister first to God, second to people, and he takes the lead in structuring services toward that end.

As you might imagine, Presence based churches and Presence based pastors must grow together—neither can really be who they are without the other. The Presence based church needs Pastor Betterdish to set the tone, to keep the Ark in the center of camp and lead by example. Although it is not built around the pastor, the Presence based church, like any organization or group, will reflect the heart of its leader in many ways. The Presence based pastor faces the unique challenge of leading his congregation with strength and decisiveness while resisting the urge to step into the limelight. He must lead from his knees, facing the cross, not the people. At times it becomes necessary for him to enforce boundaries or deliver correction in order to preserve the Presence as the focal point. He can only do this effectively if he is completely surrendered to God and in constant communication with him.

He must lead from his knees, facing the cross, not the people.

Pastor Betterdish, on the other hand, needs the prayers and blessing of the people to be a man or woman of God. The church must release him from the expectations that go along with trying to keep people happy and willingly commission him to draw apart regularly. That's not as easy as it may seem. The people must want a shepherd that is hearing from God more than they want a chaplain to watch over and tend to their personal needs. Without their encouragement and support to be a God seeker, the pastor will become entangled in daily workings that will dominate his time and drain his energy.

Pastor Betterdish knows that if he can stay in the Presence and lead his congregation to minister first and foremost to God, the typical church "people" issues will take care of themselves. However, he recognizes that the needs of his people are important so he trains leaders around him to minister to those who need comfort and counsel. The strong personal prayer ministry that we talked about in the last chapter is one of the reasons Pastor Betterdish is able to spend time in the "throne zone" without feeling guilty because he knows his people are being taken care of by trained prayer partners.

Moses was the epitome of the Presence based pastor, strong and unshakable with the Israelites, humble and contrite before God. No one questioned why he stayed on the mountain for days at a time, nor why he wasn't involved in their personal lives. They expected him to be with God, and in return he interceded on their behalf and faithfully brought them God's instructions and guidance.

Even Jesus practiced being in the Presence, often retreating alone to pray and fellowship with the Father (Mark 1:35-37). It was in these quiet moments and prolonged periods of seeking that the Presence was released in him for the work of ministry. He prayed to know the will of God, and for the power and perseverance to carry it out. He was God's representative to the people, and he related the Father's heart to them.

Presence Drawn

Whom do you live to please? The answer tells you who or what controls your life. If you aim to please your boss, then your work life will control you. If you want above all to please your spouse, then he or she has control over you. If your heart's desire is to please God, then God will be in control of your life.

The control issues so rampant in the consumer based church are minimized in the Presence based church because Jesus is the focus of attention, not the people. In the consumer based church, the goal is to gain the allegiance of as many consumers as possible by doing whatever it takes to attract their attention and ultimately meet their needs so they will stay. By trying to please them, the Martha church inadvertently gives people power to control.

In the Mary church, however, people have little leverage because the church does not revolve around their happiness. Jesus is the center of attention, and therefore he is in control. While the pastor and leadership want to be sensitive to the feelings of the congregation, those feelings are not allowed to overshadow the leading of the Holy Spirit. Pastor Betterdish and his team of leaders are Presence drawn, and the people can choose to pick up an oar and row or get off the boat. If that sounds harsh, remember that the Israelites faced the same choice. Either they submitted to Moses' leadership and fell in line, or they suffered serious consequences (unnatural death). There really wasn't much room for disagreement in the Presence.

In the Mary church people have little leverage because the church does not revolve around their happiness.

Just as the Israelites followed the cloud, the Presence based church is drawn, not driven. It always puts the Ark, Jesus, in front and follows his lead. The Presence is their guide and their governor. The accountability structure of the church at all levels honors and values the Presence above anything else. It overshadows ritual and tradition and permeates every aspect of church life—education, fellowship, family life, budget, location, staffing, preaching, worship, witness, small groups and maintenance.

If humility is the one character trait that most Presence based pastors share, then discernment, or the ability to hear the voice of God, is the distinguishing spiritual gift. They are in love with hearing the voice of God, and they inspire this same sentiment in their churches. I don't mean to say that all Presence based pastors necessarily possess a supernatural ability to hear more or better than the rest of us. But the many, many hours they spend seeking the heart of God hones their listening skills and creates a fine tuned sensitivity to the Holy Spirit's whisper. It is their relentless pursuit of the Presence that sharpens their spiritual ears and enables them to be Presence drawn leaders. As Jesus said, "My sheep listen to my voice; I know them, and they follow me" (John 10:27).

Pastor Betterdish seeks God's direction in every church decision, both large and small. His desire is that the indwelling of the Presence in their midst would control every thought and guide every step. He and his leaders ask God, "What is your plan for our church? Where would you have us go next?" and then wait for him to answer. They don't move without a mandate from the Presence.

Charles Olsen, in his book *Transforming Church Boards*, describes the difficult nature of leading by discernment by comparing it to the work of an archeologist who does not create nor destroy, but who discovers and uncovers what is already there. He says, "Consulting Scripture, waiting in silence, and corporate soul searching are not an 'easy way out.' Efficiency-minded boards are accustomed to controlling the agenda, but the discernment agenda tends to have a life of its own." He defines discernment this way:

> Discernment is not to be equated with consensus decision making. Discernment is not a political process. Discernment is not a logical, rational, ordered

discipline that leads deductively to inescapable conclusions. It is a sometimes lengthy, sometimes meandering activity of determining what God wants, or from an eternal perspective, what already is.[2]

The book Olsen wrote was actually the product of a study he led on the ways in which congregations make decisions. He found that efforts to seek and discern God's will were noticeably lacking among most church boards. The writer of the article Eric Reed comments:

> Most church leadership teams assume God is guiding what they do. But—with the influence of business models (*consumer based thinking*) on church planning and administration—the plans God has for a congregation are sometimes bypassed for the sake of efficiency (italics mine).[3]

Ephesians 2:10 says that "we are God's workmanship, created in Christ Jesus to do good works, which God prepared in advance for us to do." The Presence based church comes into the Presence to worship God, and in doing so, invites him to call them up into the work he has already prepared for them. They do not always assume that their work is his work.

Adam Hamilton, pastor of United Methodist Church of the Resurrection in Leawood, Kansas wants his church to be Presence drawn. He explains:

> Before I begin writing my sermons each week, I walk through the sanctuary and touch each section of chairs, then sit and pray, "Lord, I yield my mind, my

thoughts, my heart, my lips, my hands, my time in research to you. Help me to know what you want to say to the people who will be sitting in these chairs this weekend."

He and his leaders also pray before the services for God to take control and for the people up front to "disappear." They want to be sensitive to the leading of the Presence, even when he wants to take them outside of their usual paths.[4]

Being led outside the church's comfort zone can be scary. The flexibility that discernment requires is often a struggling point for pastors, especially those in the mainline traditions. One Baptist pastor describes his own experience with being Presence drawn:

> My seminary professor taught us how to time services down to the half-minute. While still in school I interned for a pastor who set a time for the service and was never off by more than 60 seconds, the whole time I served there. Then I took an associate position at a church and worked with a senior [pastor] who ran the service like a military operation. Again, there was no slack. I was trained to figure out what you're gonna do and then you do it, just as you planned. Any interference was not God's way of doing things.
>
> So naturally I came here and my tendency was to agonize over every minute of the service and have very tight control on timing. But then the Holy Spirit

started working in me and, before you know it, I was convinced and then I persuaded the staff and elders that we needed to be open to the Holy Spirit visiting us in some unusual ways. None of us, myself included, were at all comfortable with this in the beginning. And you know, we're pretty by the book, but once we made the shift [to greater flexibility] some very powerful things have happened.

One Sunday I was totally convinced that the Holy Spirit was calling upon me not to preach my sermon. Now is that blasphemy to a Baptist preacher or what? But instead the Spirit was pushing me to lead us in a concert of prayer. I wish you could have seen me up there. It must have looked like I was schizophrenic, wrestling with my two minds that morning. [Here he imitated the two voices that were struggling inside of him.] "I have to preach;" "I can't preach." "God wouldn't want His people to go home without exposure to His Word;" "His people don't need that today, they need something else." "This church counts on me to provide a strong message every week;" "this church hired you to lead them in ways that honor God," and so on. I tell you what, we did that morning of prayer and people were just being blessed left and right. At the end of the morning we had an altar call, which was really odd because three-quarters of 'em was already kneeling in the aisles or on the platform steps, and we had more commitments that morning than at any other service that year. Our services usually run about 75 minutes, but that one ran close to two hours.

I'm telling you, there were some miracles that morning—and none of them would have happened if I'd stuck to the plan and I'd preached my message. I am a firm—and I mean firm—believer in staying tuned into the Holy Spirit, even if it's not popular among a lot of my colleagues. I've seen what God can do when you're on His page instead of your own. But it really does take a lot of courage and getting used to.[5]

I so appreciated the honesty and candor of that story when I read it. What could be a better testimony to the power of being Presence drawn than a Baptist preacher turned radical? I can empathize with his internal conflict, and know many pastors who have gone through the very same struggle. Being Presence based is not easy because it requires a huge amount of faith and sometimes challenges the training and experience many of us have leaned on for years.

The rewards, however, are well worth the risk. Those who enter into the Presence find a divine rest that only comes from being voice activated. In the Presence, we can cease our labor, we can stop pushing, and we are not driven. The rest of God carries us. Watchman Nee has an interesting way of putting it. He says, "Christianity begins not with a big DO, but with a big DONE. Thus Ephesians opens with the statement that God has 'blessed us with every spiritual blessing in the heavenly places in Christ' (1. 3) and we are invited at the very outset to sit down and enjoy what God has done for us; not to set out to try and attain it for ourselves."[6] As we allow the Presence to lead us, we can rest in knowing that he will take us to the destiny he has already prepared for us and the blessings he has already set aside.

Divine Habitation

The rest of God doesn't come overnight. Neither does a church become Presence based overnight. It is a process and a lifelong journey requiring endurance. God's decision to abide in a place depends, to some degree, on his sovereignty, and can not be manipulated by a formula. But persistent seeking and exposure to the Presence and the smile of God will eventually create a divine habitation in which the Spirit takes up residence. God richly rewards those who hunger after him, not just in a moment of desperation, or in a time of need, but day after day, week after week and year after year, just because he is worthy.

When the Presence begins to live in our midst, his influence and favor gains control over our minds—I call it "Presence of mind." Our thinking becomes a citadel of his control. He gains a foothold in human affairs and deliberations. His authority rests on leaders, and as a result we can rest in his favor and delight in his nearness. We don't have to be in control because we are secure in him.

In a divine habitation, Jesus becomes the chief source of provision, protection, joy, correction and power. Every aspect of church life has more to do with him than with people. His hand turns the wheel and produces kingdom results, and we are privileged to participate and enjoy. Divine habitations lead to *divine strongholds* that we see in the form of sustained moves of God. Churches, ministries or individuals that are consistently producing significant fruit, powerful regional revivals and dynamic city transformations are all results of divine strongholds that were invited by a body of believers hungry enough for the Presence that they grabbed hold and wouldn't let go. That is why Presence based churches tend to rise to the surface as change agents in their community, city or even nation. They don't necessarily have to be large or well known, but they are God's resting place and a center of spiritual activity.

> God richly rewards those who hunger after him, not just in a moment of desperation, or in a time of need, but day after day, week after week and year after year, just because he is worthy.

If being Presence based leads to the establishment of divine strongholds in a church, then being consumer based contributes to the growth of *carnal strongholds* that undermine the church's effectiveness. If the enemy can keep us bickering about who should be doing what in the kitchen, or suck us into the vortex of decision making and fundraising for a building program, then he needn't worry too much about the Great Commission tally. When people are in control, Jesus isn't, and the devil can feel pretty good about that. The consumer based church gives the illusion of productivity in man-centered busyness that produces little. We get worried and distracted about many things, when only one thing is really needed.

The book of Acts is not meant to be just an historical accounting of the birth of Christianity and spread of the early church. It was meant to be an example of how the church should function as a divine habitation, and how it can grow exponentially when Jesus is the clear and uncluttered message. The disciples, an unimpressive group by their own cultural standards, had no material resources and a lousy image. They were uneducated and not especially well mannered. They had no statement of purpose and no political connections.

But none of that mattered because their personalities were hidden behind the profound power of God's message being spoken through them. The church grew in grace, truth and love. And numbers. They grew by the hundreds and even thousands as they proclaimed Jesus and ministered personally to people in his name. "The Lord's hand was with them, and a great number of people believed and turned to the Lord" (Acts 2:11). They were Presence captured (Acts 2), Presence energized (Act 4:33) and Presence drawn (Acts 8:4).

The disciples certainly didn't dedicate their lives to ministry because of the salary or retirement package. They lived on very little and most of them died martyrs' deaths. No one in that day named a church after them or even gave them a plaque. Their inheritance in heaven must be amazing though, for the lives they touched, the souls they invited into eternity, and the profound impact they had on the world, even to the end of the ages. As he was for the Levites, God was their reward. His Presence with them walking, talking, laughing and living was enough to sustain their passion even to the death.

Summary

We can complete our diagram of the Presence based church by adding four final characteristics:

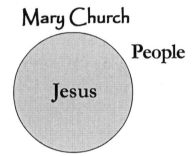

Presence Based Church

1. Levitical Worship

2. First Love Prayer

3. Compassion

4. Presence Evangelism

5. Revelation of Jesus

6. Pastor Betterdish

7. Humility

8. Presence Drawn Leadership

9. Divine Habitation

Discussion Questions

1. Can you think of a person who has many reasons to be proud (power, authority, talent, influence), yet is very humble? Describe them.

2. Why is humility such an important trait in the Presence based church? Name at least three reasons.

3. Compare and contrast Pastor Fetch and Pastor Betterdish. How are they the most alike? How are they the most different?

4. Discuss why Presence based churches and Presence based pastors must "grow together."

4. Think of a time when you felt "driven." Think of a time when you felt "drawn." What is the difference?

5. If Peter, Paul and some of the other disciples were to visit your church this Sunday, what do you think they would talk about over lunch?

6. Can you cite examples of divine habitations or divine strongholds? Explain why you think they classify.

7. What can you do as an individual to help your church become more Presence based?

EPILOGUE
WASTED ON HIM

The sisters Martha and Mary, true to character, appear a third and final time in the New Testament. Shortly after Jesus had raised Lazarus from the dead, they all found themselves in Bethany again days before the Passover and impending crucifixion. A dinner was being given in Jesus' honor at the home of a man that Matthew's and Mark's gospels call Simon the Leper.

The scene as we read it in John 12:1-8 (see also Matthew 26:6-13 and Mark 14:3-9) is full of dramatic irony because while we know in hindsight that Jesus is about to die, no one else in the story does. The people around Jesus at this time, his closest friends and disciples, don't understand that they are all players in God's cosmic salvation plan, caught up in the single most important and dramatic moment in history. Yet each of them plays his role faithfully, pushing the sequence of events to its necessary conclusion.

Martha, we are told, was serving. How very Martha. Even in someone else's house she was doing what Martha did best—being a good hostess and attending to the details of the occasion. Mary, on the other hand, was doing what Mary did best—expressing her love and devotion to Jesus.

The Bible tells us that after they had finished eating and were still reclining around the table, Mary brought out a personal jar of very expensive perfume, "poured it on Jesus' feet and wiped his feet with her hair" (John 12:3). It was a scandalous thing to do for two reasons. First, the perfume was worth about a year's wages, a huge sum of money considering the relative financial status of the group. Several of the disciples, including Judas who was ironically the official treasurer, were indignant at the waste of such a precious substance. They rebuked Mary, asking, "Why wasn't this perfume sold, and the money given to the poor?" indicating that doing so would have been consistent with the groups' ministry style.

Judas especially didn't appreciate the significance of her lavish gesture because, as his words and actions revealed, he really had no concept of who Jesus was. John lets us in on his own secret in hindsight that in addition to being the one who would betray Jesus to the authorities, Judas was also a thief who had been stealing from the money bag. It is no wonder Mary's extravagant act of love did not meet with his approval.

Mary's action also would have raised eyebrows for another

reason—it was considered improper for a woman to let her hair down in public, particularly in the presence of a man. A woman's long hair was her glory; however, propriety dictated that it always be tied or put up except when in private. Only a prostitute or woman of loose morals would have considered loosening her hair among guests at a dinner.

Mary, however, didn't care about social customs or even her own image when it came to Jesus. The extraordinary love she had for him in her heart was stronger and more compelling than any other concern. For Mary, Jesus' acceptance and validation of her unusual act of worship was all that mattered. He defended her, as he had done before, because her unbridled adoration ministered to him in a way that no one else imagined, even Mary herself.

The depth of Mary's spiritual perception of Jesus is unmatched, even among his trusted disciples. Her action stands apart all the more in light of their response to it. Even they, his inner circle of companions who had traveled with and observed the Savior up close for three years, didn't really comprehend Jesus' divinity to the extent that Mary did. She "got" him, and the weight of the revelation drove her to his feet every time she saw him.

Oh that all of us could worship him like Mary, without the constraints of pride and self-consciousness! Robert Stearnes believes that as we see a resurgence of the end time Levites, we will:

> [T]he heart of Mary will be released, and we will sit at His feet and know the penetrating gaze of His blazing eyes. Consuming us, He will be our all in all.

The alabaster box of our lives will be gladly broken, and the fragrant oil of our lives, wasted on Him, will fill the air. Presence will be valued over service. Brokenness over productivity. Intimacy over conquest."[1]

The Presence based church, like Mary, "gets" Jesus at a whole different level—it is a church so overwhelmed by the revelation of his Presence in their midst that they can't help falling at his feet in worship at every opportunity. They share with Jesus a unique love relationship. They don't count the cost nor worry over their own reputation as they lavish upon him their love and adoration. They are the offering, humbled and smitten by the Lord of glory. So extravagant is their love that they will expend any or all of their resources just to minister to him. In return, Jesus defends the Presence based church and bestows on it his favor and blessing. It is special to him because it ministers to him in a way that only he really understands.

As churches, we don't know what part we are playing in the cosmic scheme of God's redemption of the world. We, like those who were with Jesus in his last days, are not able to see the significance of our own actions. But what if we were? What if we could step off the stage and into the audience and watch our own contribution, knowing the full details of the end of the story. Would we more readily pour out our love on him and spend ourselves in worship if we could *really* see him for who he is? Would we sing to him?

Like oil upon your feet

Like wine for you to drink

Like water from my heart
I'll pour my love on you.
If praise is like perfume
I'll lavish mine on you
'Til every drop is gone
I'll pour my love on you.[2]

Read the end of the story—Christianity culminates in a great and powerful expression of worship that engulfs all of heaven and earth. Everything *will* praise him and people will encounter him as never before. Kings, celebrities, diplomats and generals will all fall face down in submission to the Lord of glory. All of life's struggles and problems, joys and accomplishments will melt away at the resplendence of the glory of Jesus Christ. He is worthy—waste yourself on Him.

Notes

Introduction
1. A. W. Tozer, *The Pursuit of God* (Camp Hill, PA: Christian Publications Inc., 1993) 67.

Chapter 2 The Consumer Based Church
1. Elmer Towns, *An Inside Look at Ten of Today's Most Innovative Churches* (Ventura, CA: Regal Books, 1990) 196.
2. Sally Morgenthaler, *Worship Evangelism* (Grand Rapids, MI: Zondervan Publishing House, 1999) 20.
3. William Easum and Thomas Bandy, *Growing Spiritual Redwoods* (Nashville, TN: Abingdon Press, 1997) 96.
4. George Barna, *The Second Coming of the Church* (Nashville, TN: Word Publishing, 1998) 72.
5. Dan Scott, *The Emerging American Church* (Anderson IN: Bristol Books, 1993) 18-19.
6. Barna, 69.
7. Barna Research Group Online, "New Book Describes the State of the Church in 2002," *Barna Updates,* June 4 2002.
8. Barna Research Group Online, "America's Faith is Changing—But Beneath the Surface," *Barna Updates,* March 18, 2003.
9. William Chadwick, *Stealing Sheep* (Downers Grove, IL: InterVarsity Press, 2001) 20.
10. Ibid., 23.
11. Ibid., 30.
12. Morgenthaler, 135-137.
13. Ibid., 36.
14. A. A. Milne, "Sneezles," *Now We Are Six,* (New York: E. P. Dutton & Company, 1955) 16.

Chapter 4 The Presence
1. Walter L. Walker, *Extraordinary Encounters with God* (Ann Arbor, MI: Servant Publications, 1997) 70.
2. *The American Heritage Dictionary of the English Language,* Fourth Edition (Boston, MA: Houghton Mifflin Company, 2000).
3. Frank Damazio, *The Gate Church* (Portland OR: City Bible Publishing, 2000) 108.
4. Philip Yancey, *The Bible Jesus Read* (Grand Rapids, MI: Zondervan Publishing House, 1999).

Chapter 5 The Ark of the Covenant

1. James Strong, *The Tabernacle of Israel* (Grand Rapids, MI: Kregel Publications, 1987) 145.
2. Rudolph Otto, *The Idea of the Holy* (Oxford University Press, 1950) 12-13.
3. R.C. Sproul, *The Fearful Mystery* (Wheaton, IL: Tyndale House Publishers, 1985) 60-61.
4. Philip Yancey, *The Jesus I Never Knew* (Grand Rapids, MI: Zondervan Publishing House, 1995) 36.

Chapter 6 Jesus – The New Ark

1. Sally Morgenthaler, *Worship Evangelism* (Grand Rapids, MI: Zondervan Publishing House, 1999) 103.
2. Philip Yancey, *The Jesus I Never Knew* (Grand Rapids, MI: Zondervan Publishing House, 1995) 36.

Chapter 7 Presence Based Worship

1. Dick Eastman, *Pathways of Delight* (Ventura, CA: Regal Books, 2002) 166-167.
2. David Watson, *I Believe in the Church* (Grand Rapids, MI: William B. Eerdmans Publishing Company, 1978) 179.
3. Jack Hayford, "Getting to the Heart of Worship," *Ministries Today*, (Sept./Oct 2003) 68.
4. Kevin Conner, *The Temple of Solomon* (Portland, OR: City Bible Publishing, 1988) 189.
5. Terry Teykl, *Making Room to Pray* (Muncie, IN: Prayer Point Press, 1993).
6. Mike Bickle, *The Pleasures of Loving God* (Lake Mary, FL: Creation House, 2000) 174.
7. Matt Redman, *The Unquenchable Worshipper* (Ventura, CA: Regal Books, 2001) 102-104.
8. Brian Doerksen, "Leading Worship in Weakness," *Worship Update*, a quarterly publication of "Touching the Father's Heart," Vineyard Music Group, vol. 3, no. 3 (Spring 1989).
9. Ron Kenoly and Dick Bernal, *Lifting Him Up* (Orlando, FL: Creation House, 1995) 23.
10. Robert Stearnes, *Prepare the Way* (Lake Mary, FL: Creation House, 1999) 7.
11. George Barna, *The Habits of Highly Effective Churches* (Ventura, CA: Regal Books, 1999) 109.
12. Sally Morgenthaler, *Worship Evangelism* (Grand Rapids, MI: Zondervan Publishing House, 1999) 23.
13. Hayford, 68.

14. Randy Harvey, senior pastor and worship leader The Crossing Church, The Woodlands, TX, personal interview, Oct. 9, 2003)

15. Joseph Garlington, *Worship: The Pattern of Things in Heaven* (Shippensburg, PA: Destiny Image Publishers, Inc., 1997) 129.

16. "Meet With Me," words and music by Ross King, from the CD *The Spirit Moves*, produced by Breakaway Ministries, College Station, TX, 2000.

Chapter 8 The New Order of Levites

1. Alfred Edersheim, *The Temple* (Peabody, MA: Hendrickson Publishers, 1994) 111.

2. George Barna, *The Habits of Highly Effective Churches* (Ventura, CA: Regal Books, 1999) 95.

3. John Piper, *Let the Nations Be Glad* (Grand Rapids, MI: Baker Book House, 1993) 11.

4. Robert Stearnes, *Prepare the Way* (Lake Mary, FL: Creation House, 1999) 165.

5. Tommy Tenney, *God Chasers* (Shippensburg, PA: Destiny Image Publishers, Inc., 1998).

6. John Wimber, "Worship: Intimacy with God," *Equipping the Saints*, (Jan/Feb 1987, vol. 1 no. 1) 4.

7. Charles Trombley, *Praise* (Indianola, IA: Fountain Press, Inc., 1978) 19-38.

8. Matt Redman, *The Unquenchable Worshipper* (Ventura, CA: Regal Books, 2001) 51.

9. William Temple, *Readings in St. John's Gospel* (Macmillan, 1939) 68.

Chapter 9 The Presence Based Church

1. C. S. Lewis, *Reflections on the Psalms* (Fontana, 1961) 80.

2. Terry Teykl, *Acts 29* (Muncie, IN: Prayer Point Press, 1999).

3. George Barna, *The Habits of Highly Effective Churches* (Ventura, CA: Regal Books, 1999) 104.

4. Steve Hawthorne and Graham Kendrick, *Prayerwalking* (Orlando, FL: Creation House, 1993) 135-136.

5. E. Stanley Jones, "How to Pray," *The Christian Advocate*, 1945.

6. Terry Teykl, *Outside the Camp* (Muncie, IN: Prayer Point Press, 2001) 13-14.

7. Oswald Chambers, *My Utmost For His Highest* (New York: Dodd, Mead & Company, 1935) 22.

8. Ed Silvoso, *Prayer Evangelism* (Ventura, CA: Regal Books, 2000).

9. David Garrett, *Global Worship Report I*, from the AD2000 Worship and Arts Network, (January 1999, no. 8).

10. Steve Macchia, *Becoming a Healthy Church* quoted by Leith Anderson, "7 Ways to Rate Your Church," *Leadership Journal* (Winter 1999) 37.

11. Tommy Tenney, *God Chasers* (Shippensburg, PA: Destiny Image Publishers, Inc., 1998) 13.

12. Jim Cymbala, *Fresh Wind, Fresh Fire* (Grand Rapids, MI: Zondervan Publishing House, 1997) 124.

13. Robert Stearnes, *Prepare the Way* (Lake Mary, FL: Creation House, 1999) 7.

14. Ibid., 7.

Chapter 10 The Presence Based Pastor

1. Jim Cymbala, *Fresh Wind, Fresh Fire* (Grand Rapids, MI: Zondervan Publishing House, 1997) 121.

2. Charles Olsen, *Transforming Church Boards* (Alban, 1995) quoted by Eric Reed, "Ask the 'God'Questions," *Leadership Journal*, (Fall 2001) 44.

3. Eric Reed, "Ask the 'God'Questions," *Leadership Journal*, (Fall 2001) 44.

4. Adam Hamilton, "Rehearsing the Covenant," *Leadership Journal*, (Fall 2001) 42.

5. Unnamed Baptist pastor quoted by George Barna, *The Habits of Highly Effective Churches* (Ventura, CA: Regal Books, 1999) 107-109.

6. Watchman Nee, *Sit, Walk, Stand* (Fort Washington, PA: Christian Literature Crusade, 1962) 12.

Epilogue Wasted on Him

1. Robert Stearnes, *Prepare the Way* (Lake Mary, FL: Creation House, 1999) 166.

2. "Pour My Love," words and music by Philips, Craig and Dean, from the CD *Let My Words be Few*, Sparrow Records, 2001.

OTHER *PRESENCE BASED CHURCH* RESOURCES

The Presence Based Church Study Journal - excellent companion to *The Presence Based Church* book. Contains topic outlines for small group study or notetaking, and journal pages for each chapter for recording thoughts, revelations and answers to chapter discussion questions.

"Martha and Mary" CD - live audio teaching by Dr. Terry Teykl on the Martha and Mary churches.

OTHER TITLES BY TERRY TEYKL

Making Room to Pray

Preyed On or Prayed For

Acts 29

Pray the Price

Blueprint for the House of Prayer

How to Pray After You've Kicked the Dog

Mosquito on an Elephant's Rump

Outside the Camp

Praying Grace

These and other resources are available through Prayer Point Press. For information or to order, call toll free 1.888.656.6067 or visit www.prayerpointpress.com.